Although the praying mantis may seem like a pet that you cannot really pet and cuddle with, you will be surprised to know how much they enjoy spending time with their owners. They are quirky little creatures and also love a lot of playtime.

So, if you want a pet that will give you hours of entertainment by climbing around the enclosure, hopping from one place to another and just gazing at you like he wants to know you better, then the praying mantis is the perfect pet for you. What's more, he will fit right into your pocket, so you can take him wherever you go. Now, that is the kind of companion that everyone needs. Please note, there are female praying mantises, however we shall refer to them as "he" for ease.

Chapter 1: About the Praying Mantis

The more you learn about the type of pet that you plan to bring home, the better care you will be able to provide. The praying mantis is an unusual pet, no doubt. In addition to this, there are several myths surrounding this tiny creature that make them seem like the least popular choice for a pet.

The truth, however, is that raising a praying mantis can be extremely fun. You just need to know what he needs in order to thrive. This knowledge begins by learning about the life history and the natural history of the praying mantis.

1. Physical appearance

Praying mantises belong to the order Mantodea, which consists of more than 2400 species of insects that are divided into 15 families. Of these, the largest family is named the Mantidae.

These insects tend to have elongated bodies and most often have no wings. One thing that is common with all the Mantodea is that they have forelegs that are very enlarged, making it suitable for them to hold and eat their prey.

When they stand in an upright position, this forearm is normally bent, making it look like they are praying. As a result, they have been given the name of praying mantis.

The first thing that you will notice about the praying mantis is the head. It is large and triangular in shape. They have a snout that almost looks like a beak and they also have mandibles. They have large, compound eyes that are bulbous, along with three other simple eyes that are smaller, and a single pair of antennae.

Praying Mantis

Praying Mantises as Pets.

Praying Mantis Owners Manual.

by

David Overtone

ALL RIGHTS RESERVED. This book contains material protected under International and Federal Copyright Laws and Treaties.

Any unauthorized reprint or use of this material is strictly prohibited. No part of this book may be reproduced or transmitted in any form or by any means, electronic, mechanical or otherwise, including photocopying or recording, or by any information storage and retrieval system without express written permission from the author.

Copyright © 2018

Published by: Zoodoo Publishing

Table of Contents

Table of Contents 3
Introduction 4
Chapter 1: About the Praying Mantis 6
Chapter 2: Top Mantis Species 21
Chapter 3: Your Pet Praying Mantis 30
Chapter 4: Praying Mantis Care 56
Chapter 5: Breeding Praying Mantises 87
Chapter 6: Health Issues in Praying Mantis 100
Conclusion 108
References 109

Introduction

Are you looking for a pet that is extremely unusual? One that does not need to be taken on walks, one with which you do not have to worry about the litter box, but can still enjoy great companionship?

Well, then the praying mantis is the perfect pet for you. These beautiful and extremely intelligent insects have been chosen as pets in many homes. They are entertaining and almost seem to understand you when you talk to them or interact with them.

Then there is the whole excitement of building a new terrarium and enclosure for your new buddy. This is a great project and can keep you busy even before your praying mantis arrives.

A praying mantis is a very easy pet to take care of. However, you need to learn a couple of things about taking care of your praying mantis before you bring one home.

This book addresses exactly that and makes sure that you have all the information that you will need in order to take care of your possible new pet. This book compiles the experiences and tips from other praying mantis owners to give you practical solutions to any roadblocks that you may face along the way.

All the details about sourcing your praying mantis, finding the right enclosure, the food that you need to provide and also healthcare for your little companion are provided in this book. For beginners, this information is very useful to improve the lifespan of the pet and to keep them healthy and happy.

Their necks are extremely flexible. In fact, in some species, these heads can rotate to 180 degrees. The thorax is divided into three parts: the prothorax, the mesothorax and the metathorax.

Except for the genus Mantoida, all species have the head and the forelegs attached to the prothorax. This segment is much longer in comparison to the other two segments. The prothorax is also very flexible and allows a wide range of movements for the forelimbs and the head.

The rest of the body of the praying mantis is almost immobile. They have grasping forelegs that are spiked. These legs, also called the raptorial legs, allow them to hold the prey securely. Just below the femur-like structure of the forelegs, these insects have a set of spines that have teeth-like tubercles. They have several other smaller tubercles along with a claw-like structure that allows the mantis to get a firm grip on any prey.

At the end of the foreleg is a delicate structure called the tarsus. This is used by the mantis to walk. This has about five segments and also a claw with two toes at the end.

There are different types of mantises based on the wings. Some are categorized as long-winged or macropterous, short winged or brachypterous, vestigial winged or micropterus, or wingless or apterous.

If the mantis is not wingless, it usually has two sets of wings. The outer set of wings is called the tegmina and they appear leathery and narrow. These wings are used by the mantis for camouflage and also to protect the next set of hind wings, which are delicate and clear in their appearance.

The male and female mantis can be distinguished by the appearance of the abdomen. It is a lot slimmer in the males when compared to the females. In addition to this, the abdomen has structures called sternites, which are visible in the males and not clearly seen in females.

Mantises have been part of folklore for several centuries. In fact, in Ancient Egypt, Greece and Assyria, it was believed that these insects also have supernatural powers. Today, praying mantises are very popular pets because they are easy to handle and are also quite entertaining to watch.

2. The Vision of Mantises

One of the most spectacular qualities of the praying mantis is their vision. These insects have simple and compound eyes that allow them to have stereovision. Because they get information from these two types of eyes, they are able to perceive depth better and also have better perception of any 3D object.

At night, they use their sight to locate their prey. Their compound eyes have about 10000 cells called ommatidia. The frontal section of the compound eye is most active. It has the ability to produce high-resolution images that can help the mantis spot any prey.

The ommatidia in the periphery of the compound eye have the ability to perceive motion, so when anything moves around the praying mantis, the eye moves swiftly to get a high resolution image of that object.

The eyes of the mantis are situated far away from each other on the sides of the head. This allows them to have a better binocular range. This also makes them have a very precise stereotypic image when the object is at a closer range.

Each eye has a dark spot that moves when the mantis rotates the head. This structure is called the pseudopupil. The movement is a result of the manner in which the ommatidia absorb and reflect light.

Since their hunting depends mostly on their vision, praying mantises are diurnal. This means that they are most active during the day. However, some species also tend to fly at night, as they are attracted to artificial light. This behavior is mostly seen in praying mantises that belong to the family Liturgusidae. Most of the specimens from this family that have been collected for research have turned out to be males. This is probably the case with most species of the praying mantis.

Male praying mantises tend to exhibit this behavior, which is also called nocturnal flight, because they are trying to located female mantises. Females are inactive during the night and this allows the males to detect the pheromones of the females easily. This helps them find a potential mate.

It also believed that praying mantises may resort to nocturnal flight as they are less vulnerable to birds and other predators at that time. Along with their vision, they also make use of an auditory organ that is located on the thorax. This functions very similarly to the echolocation call that is used by bats to find their way around in the dark.

3. Taxonomy

Currently, over 2400 species of Praying mantises have been recognized. These have been categorized into 430 genera. Most of these species have been found in the tropical regions while some of them are also native to temperate regions. The classification of these insects has been debated for several years.

Initially, they were classified under Phasmatodea with stick insects. Then they were classified under the order Orthoptera along with cockroaches. Then, they were classified under the order Grylloblattodea along with rock crawlers.

In the year 1991, the order Mantodea was combined with termites and cockroaches into the order dictyoptera, the suborder Mantodea.

The word *Mantodea*has been formed by combining two Ancient Greek words. The first one is *mantis,* which means "prophet" and the second one is *edios,* which means "type or form".

This term was coined in the year 1838 by Hermann Burmeister, a German entomologist. Occasionally, this order is also known as mantes, which is the Latin plural version of the Greek word *mantis.*

Commonly, this insect is known as the praying mantis and the name is applied to all species that belong to this order. This is because of the posture of the forelimbs that seem to be folded in prayer. In the USA, the plural used is mantises while in the UK and in other parts of the world, the term mantids is used commonly.

In the year 1968, a proposition was made to split the family Mantidae into 8 separate families. However, these families were further reclassified to form 15 families in the year 2002. This was when this idea of classifying under multiple families was adopted universally.

In the year 1997, a study of the external genitalia of the male mantises revealed that the families Metallyticidae and Chaeteessidae had divergerd from other families much earlier. However, since the Thespidae and Mantidae are still believed to be polyphyletic, the suborder Mantodea must be revised.

Some of the earliest fossils of mantises were recovered from Siberia. These fossils date back 135 million years. The fossils of this group are very rare. By 2007, there were only 25 species of fossils that were known. Some of these fossils found in Cretaceous amber, including a fossil from Japan, have revealed that these creatures had spines on the forelimbs just like the modern day Mantis. While most of the fossils found in amber are ones of nymphs, whereas fossils of adults have been observed in rocks.

Some of these fossils, that have been uncovered in the Crato formation, Brazil also include the *Santanmantisaxelrodi*. The description of these fossils reveal that they also had front legs that were adapted to catch prey. There are several small specimens that have been preserved quite well. They reveal several details when observed with X-ray tomography.

It is possible to confuse the mantis with mantidflies because they both have similar forelimbs. However, these two creatures are unrelated. This similarity in the structure of the forelimbs is a result of evolution. However, the mantidflies do not have the leathery forewings. They have shorter antennae that are not thread like. Themantidflies also tend to tip back a little more before they catch their prey when compared to the praying mantis.

4. Praying mantis adaptations

Mantises are food for several vertebrates such as birds, frogs and lizards. They are also preyed on by several species of spiders and ants. There are some species of hunting wasps as well that tend to paralyze the praying mantis in order to feed the young.

This is why mantises have developed several ways of protecting themselves and have made quite a few adaptations.

- **Camouflage:** This is the first method of defense. It is a common method that is used by most insects. They blend in with the foliage or the background that they reside in because of the coloration of their bodies.

  Camouflage is not only used to keep predators at bay but is also used by them to catch their own prey. Even the bodies of these insects are shaped to match their surroundings. For instance, the mantises that live on surfaces that are uniformly colored tend to have a flattened dorso-ventral shape. This includes surfaces like tree barks and even barren land. That way, even the shadow of the mantis is not seen.

Then, you have some species that are called flower mantises. These species are extremely aggressive in their mimicry of their surroundings. They look so similar to the flowers that they are able to attract their prey that mistake them for flowers and come to them to collect nectar and pollen.

In Australia and Africa, there are some species that have the ability to turn black in color. This happens as the dry season comes to an end when the mantis molts. This is when there are bush fires and the mantis blends in perfectly to the landscape that is fire ravaged.

- **Bluffing:** When a praying mantis is threatened directly, he tries to ward it off by looking larger. He fans his wings out and spreads his forelegs as he stands tall. When the wings are fanned out, the mantis looks a lot more threatening. There are bright patterns and colors in the inner surface of the forelimbs and on the wings of some species. This makes them look a lot more threating

If the predator further harasses the mantis, it is possible that he also produces a hissing sound by shooting air out of the abdomen. Mantises are not poisonous and have no way of defending themselves chemically. This is why they make use of bluffing to escape any threat.

At night, it is possible for some species to make use of echolocation to get their way around. Whenever the frequency is too high, it indicates that a bat or some predator is approaching. This is when the mantises stop flying in a horizontal direction and begin their descent towards the ground. Sometimes, they may also display some spins or aerial loops before doing this. In case the mantis is caught as he descends, he can slash the predator with the forelegs.

- **Body movements:** Just like stick insects, mantises also make use of side-to-side movements that are rhythmic and repetitive. This movement resembles the movement of leaves or trees when it is windy.

This swaying movement is also a way for the mantis to differentiate between different things in their background. This is a visual mechanism that is used by several animals.

The swaying movement then changes into running or flying depending upon the movement of the object that they are following in their visual field.

5. Life history of the praying mantis

In temperate climates, praying mantises usually breed in autumn. In the case of tropical areas, there is no fixed breeding period. Mating begins with a courtship ritual.

When mating, the male mounts the back of the female and clasps the base of the wings and the thorax with the forelegs. The male arches forward from the abdomen towards a special chamber located at the female's abdomen and deposits the sperms.

Following mating, the female mantis may lay between 10 to 400 eggs. This depends on the species of the mantis. The eggs are laid with an enclosure of froth mass. This froth mass is produced by certain glands located in the abdomen. This enclosure hardens with time to create a capsule that protects the eggs. This entire structure is called the ootheca.

The ootheca may be laid on the ground, attached to the abdomen or even wrapped around a tree depending on the species of the mantis.

There are several types of parasitic wasps that tend to feed on this ootheca. This is why they are never fully protected despite the covering. In the case of some species of bark and ground mantises, the eggs are protected by the mother. This behavior is very common in mantises belonging to the Tarachodidae family.

For instance, in the case of one species called the *Tarachodesmarurus,* the mother positions herself on the bark in such a way that the eggs are covered by her abdomen. Then, in case any predator approaches the eggs, she ambushes it. She stays in this position until the eggs hatch.

The Brunner's stick mantis adopts a reproductive strategy that is rather strange. The females do not need a male sperm to fertilize the egg. This means that reproduction happens through a process known as parthogenesis. This behavior is also seen in the *Miomantis* and the *sphodromantisvirdis.* These two species also reproduce sexually. In areas that have temperate weather conditions, the adults usually do not make it through the harsh winters. The eggs become dormant and hatch later on during the spring season.

Just like any other insect species that is closely related, praying mantises also go through three stages of life:

- The egg
- The nymph
- The adult

Insects that go through these stages of development are classified as hemimetabolous insects. In the case of smaller species of praying mantises, the eggs typically hatch in about 3-4 weeks. In the case of larger species, this can take up to 4-6 weeks.

When the nymph grows in size, the exoskeleton molts. It is possible that molting occurs about 5- 10 times before the nymph becomes an adult. Once the final molt is done, most species develop wings. It is possible that some of them are born without wings. Most often, the females are wingless.

The species of mantis determines the life span. While some of them live for just about 4-8 weeks, others may live as long as 4-8 months.

6. Praying mantises and humans

Long before they were kept as pets, praying mantises were admired for their agility and beauty and were a big part of human culture. They have had a place in our folklore, literature and much more.

Humans and praying mantises have been associated in different ways for centuries. Here is proof that praying mantises have intrigued human beings since time immemorial.

Praying mantis in art and literature

The earliest known reference to the praying mantis is in *Erya,* which is the Chinese dictionary. The attributes of the mantis have been described through poetry. The poem talks of the fearlessness and courage of the insect and then goes on to describe the physical appearance as well.

In the year 1108, a text named *JingshiZhengleiDauguanBencao* talks very precisely about the anatomy, the egg packages, the development cycle and other characteristics of the praying mantis.

There is very little mention of the praying mantis in Ancient Greek literature. However, in silver coins that were minted in the 5th century BC, illustrations of a female praying mantis in an attacking posture have been seen. These illustrations were also seen in other Greek currency units known as dirachms.

In the 10th century AD, there have been mentions of an insect that looks like a locust, but moves slowly and has long front legs in *Adages* from the Byzantine era by Suidas. The word *seriphos* has been used to denote the mantis. The word *graus* means old woman and has been used to describe the dry, stick-like body of the mantis.

There have also been several Western descriptions that give detailed information about the morphology and the biology of the praying mantis. The most accurate records date back to the 18th century. The praying mantis has been described and even illustrated in *Insketen-Belugstigungen* by Rosel von Rosenhof. He also talks about cannibalism, which is very common with these insects.

In his novel, *Island,* published in the year 1962, Aldous Huxley provides philosophical insights about death with his description of two mantises that mated before two characters in the novel.

The autobiographical book by Gerald Durrell, a naturalist, titled *My family and other animals,* was published in 1956. This book carries four long pages of a battle between a gecko and a mantis that was evenly matched.

The *Dream,* a woodcut by M.C Escher, carries the illustration of a mantis that is as large as a human. This mantis stands on the body of a bishop who is sleeping. A film named *The Deadly Mantis* released in the year 1957 features a mantis in the form of a giant monster.

The female praying mantis has always been named a *femme fatale.* This is a popular idea that was propagated in several cartoons by Guy and Rodd, Mark Parisi, Lievre and several others.

In the year 2008, a short film on praying mantises was made by Isabella Rosselini for the Sundance Channel as well.

Mantises inspire martial arts
In China, two forms of martial arts have based their fight strategies and movements on the ones used by the praying mantis. One of these martial arts was primarily practiced in the northern parts of China and is called the "Northern Praying Mantis". The other one was developed in the southern part and is called the "Southern Praying Mantis"

Both forms are extremely popular and have also been passed on to the Western world over the decades.

Praying Mantises in religion and mythology
The African San and Khoi cultures have revered the praying mantis for decades. These cultures, predominant in the southern parts of Africa, believe that humans and nature are very closely related.

The praying mantis is revered for its peculiar posture and was named the Hottentotsgot. This translates to "God of the Khoi" from Afrikaans. This language was developed by the early European settlers in Africa.

In San culture, there are references to a trickster deity who assumed many forms such as a vulture, snake, hare and even the praying mantis.

There are records of several ancient civilizations that believed that these insects possessed supernatural powers. The Greeks believed that lost travelers could find their way home with the help of a praying mantis.

A reference in the *Book of the Dead* from Ancient Egypt refers to the praying mantis as the "bird fly". This minor god was responsible for carried the souls of the deceased to the underworld.

Ancient Assyrian texts dating back to the 9th century BC believe that mantises had the power to communicate with the dead. They were also referred to as soothsayers in several contexts.

Praying Mantis as pets
Today praying mantises are among the most popular choice for pets, among other types of insects. They are in fact the most widely found type of insects kept as pets.

In many cases, people who keep mantises also breed them. This is because these creatures live for less than a year. A study conducted in the United Kingdom in 2013 revealed that close to 31 species of praying mantises were kept as pets and also bred. This was true even in the Netherlands and the United States.

By the year 1996, close to 50 species of praying mantises were bred in captivity by a group called the Mantis Study Group. Several popular articles about these creatures were carried in popular publications, too.

According to the *Independent,* praying mantises were like the stick insect, only with the touch of a Buddhist monk. The articles talked about caring for these creatures and also mentioned that they require a vivarium that measures 12 inches on all sides.

An article in *The Daily south* compared the praying mantis to other popular or "weird" choices for pets such as the ferret and the rat. However, the article stated that they do not shed, bark and do not need a litter box or shots.

Praying mantises in pest control
Several programs have been conducted globally to introduce farmers and gardeners to the benefits of using praying mantises in agriculture. For farmers and gardeners who prefer not to use any chemical based pesticides, especially, these insects are extremely valuable to keep pests at bay.

However, these insects have not yet become entirely popular with respect to agriculture because they do not have a few attributes that are common with agents used for biological pest control. These insects do not multiply with an increase in pests and cannot be used to get rid of a particular type of pest.

These insects are regular predators. They will catch just about anything that they can find to eat. This, in some cases, even includes insects that are actually beneficial for farming and agriculture.

However, several attempts are still being made to increase the importance of praying mantises in biological pest control because they are widely found. Two species of praying mantises, namely the European and Chinese praying mantis, were introduced in North

America to promote their importance in pest control. They have become quite popular in Canada and the United States today.

Praying mantises inspire technology of the future
Praying mantises could be the inspiration behind breakthrough technology in robotics. One issue faced by modern robotics is the ability to judge distance correctly. This issue, as claimed by British scientists, can easily be solved by taking a few hints from the movements of the praying mantis.

Even the "vision" of a robot could be more accurate when based on the vision of praying mantises. Today, most of this technology is based on the stereovision that humans are capable of.

The two eyes of humans receive different visual stimuli or images. These are merged in the brain to create a perception of depth. This method, however, does not seem to work in case of artificial intelligence. In fact, this only makes them slower in terms of processing time.

Some researchers from Newcastle University turned to other types of stereovision and found that the praying mantis fit the bill perfectly. In fact, it is the only insect that possesses this type of vision.

These insects judge distance based on the movement of the object. This simple form of stereovision can help reduce computing time in robots and can make them a lot more accurate as well.

So you see, there are several reasons why the praying mantis has fascinated mankind for centuries. If you are planning to bring one home, you can be assured of a great pet that is fun and extremely entertaining.

Like any other pet, the praying mantis has a few requirements that you have to take care of. Read on to learn more about how you can keep a praying mantis at home and take good care of him as well.

Chapter 2: Top Mantis Species

There are thousands of praying mantis species, but some of them are more well known than others. Knowing the species will tell you what to expect in terms of the lifespan, the diet and several other characteristics.

1.Top 5 Mantis Species

Here are the top 5 species of praying mantises that are most often kept as pets:

Chinese mantis

Scientific name: *TendoraSinenisis*

Ease of breeding: Easy to moderate

Group Housing: No

Ideal temperature requirement: 22-30 degree C. Must not go below 8 degree C.

Appearance: Chinese Mantises are very easy to identify. These are following characteristics of the Chinese Mantis:

- The body and the wings are brown in color while the wings have a green edge.

- The shape of the body is like a regular mantis and does not have any appendages that are too decorative.

- An adult Chinese mantis will grow up to 4 inches in length.

- Even the young mantis or the nymph is brown in color and does not have any special appendages.

- The female is much larger and heavier than the male and the two genders appear almost the same for the most part of their lives. The only difference between the male and the female is the antennae, with the male having longer antennae.

Why they make great pets

- They are the most common species kept as pets and are, hence, easy to find.

- They are large enough to handle easily.

- They do not need as much humidity and can adapt to most temperatures.

- All you need to do is spray the enclosure with water about 2 to 3 times each week.

- They are very easy to feed. They will eat a variety of foods from moths, flies, morio worms to roaches.

- The nymphs only need small crickets and fruit flies.

- They are very entertaining to have as pets as they hunt their prey before eating.

The downsides:
- They are not the best looking mantises.

- They are usually brown colored.

- They do not camouflage as well.

Giant Asian Mantis

Scientific name: *Hierodulamembranacea*

Ease of breeding: Easy

Group Housing: No

Ideal Temperature: 24 degree Celsius during the day and about 17 degrees C at night.

Appearance: The unique appearance of these mantises makes them very popular pets. Here are some interesting traits of the Great Asian Mantis:

- The body of this mantis is generally green in color but it is also available in brown and beige varieties. Some of the beige Asian Mantises have a pinkish tinge.

- The color of the body depends on the temperature conditions and the environmental conditions of this species.

- In just a few days, the color of the mantis can change very easily. However, there is no clear understanding of how the color of this mantis changes.

- This is one of the largest species of praying mantises. The adults can grow up to 5 inches in length and the males are usually 3 inches long.

- The male is also slender in comparison to the female. The males have wings that extend beyond the body while females have shorter wings and a shorter structure overall.

Why they make great pets:

- They are large and very beautiful to look at.

- They are very easy to take care of. They can adapt to almost all temperatures.

- All you have to do is spray the enclosure with water 2 to 3 times each day.

- They are very easy to feed. They can be given anything from crickets and roaches to flies.

- Even the nymphs feed on large insects like crickets.

The downside:
- These mantises are not very easily available.

- They are susceptible to common mantis food infections.

Budwing mantis

Scientific name: *Parasphendaleaffins/ Parasphedaleargrionina*

Ease of breeding: Easy

Group Housing: No

Ideal temperature: The ideal temperature conditions for this mantis are between 24 degrees C and 30 degrees C.

Appearance: These mantises are among the few mantises that have patterns on the body. Here are some characteristics that will help you identify them:

- The color of these mantises varies from light brown to medium brown normally. They also come in beige and extremely dark variations. The legs and the body are covered with light and dark spots.

- The females of this species are about 7 cms long while the males are only about 4 cms in length.

- Adult females do sprout wings but usually have very short ones that do not allow them to fly easily. The wings only reach up to half the abdomen of the female.

- The wings of the female are used for diematic display. This means that she will put her wings up and show off the underside, which is brightly colored. The underside of the wing comes in colors like bright orange and yellow.

- Even the inside of the legs of this mantis species is colored brightly. It has hues of yellow and orange that help the mantis ward off predators.

- In some varieties the underside of the wing may also be completely black with distinct pink colored veins.

- Males on the other hand have wings that are very long, usually extending beyond the length of the body.

- Males use the wings primarily for flight and do not showcase any diematic display.

Why they make good pets

- They are extremely interesting pets.

- Female budwing mantises can be very ferocious and can keep even large, insect-eating birds away from their space.

- They are also very good-looking creatures with bright patterns on the body.

The downside:

- They are harder to take care of in comparison to the mantises mentioned above.

African Mantis

Scientific name: *Sphodromantislineola*

Ease of breeding: Moderate

Group Housing: No

Ideal Temperature: The ideal temperature is 25 degrees C, although they can survive in a range of temperatures varying from 24 degrees C to 30 degrees C.

Appearance: Originating in the sub-Sahara regions, this variety of mantis is relatively easy to identify. The typical characteristics of this mantis are as follows:

- The color of the mantis can vary between brown and beige, although they are primarily black in color.

- The color difference in this species of mantis is mostly because of the changes in the environment of the mantis.

- The most striking feature of the mantis, especially the brown varieties, is the color of their eyes. They have striking purple eyes.

- This is a large species of mantis of which the female can grow up to 8 cms in length while the males usually grow up to 6 or 7 cms in length.

- The wings of the male are much thinner in comparison to the female but are longer, reaching to just about the tip of the body.

- The females have smaller wings that grow a little less in length in comparison to the males. The females usually have yellow colored dots on the wings.

Why they make great pets

- They are very easy to care for.

- They do not need any special temperature and do not need high humidity either.

The downside

- Since they are smaller mantises, they are not bred by many breeders.

- They are also quite boring as pets.

Ghost mantis

Scientific name: *Phyllocraniaparadoxa*
Ease of breeding: Easy

Group housing: Yes

Ideal temperature: 26 degrees Celsius. However, they may survive in temperatures between 20 and 30 degrees C.

Appearance: These mantises always live among withered leaves and have traits that mimic the environment perfectly. The unique characteristics of this mantis are as follows:

- The body resembles withered leaves and the whole body is covered with decorations that look exactly like leaves.

- The head of this mantis has a very distinct triangular shape that distorts the body to make it look exactly like a leaf.

- These mantises normally live in forests in Africa and Madagascar among withered leaves, which is their natural habitat.

- These mantises are excellent predators, as they are not seen by most of their prey. They can even devour some large species of insectivorous birds.

- These mantises are usually dark brown in color. However, depending on the environment, they can also be light brown or even green in color at times.

- When they are in more humid conditions, they tend to be greener in color.

- These mantises usually grow up to 5 cms in length and there is no distinct difference in size between the male and the female.

- The males will have thinner wings that are longer than their body while the females tend to have bodies that are bulkier and wider.

- The females have a prothorax that is wider, and the wings are shorter, too.

- You can also see the difference in the genders in this species when they are in the nymph stage, with the males having extensions on the head that are more intended.

Why they make the best pets

- They are extremely easy to handle.

- You can also keep them in groups without hassle.

The downside

- They are harder to find in the pet trade.

- These mantises need higher temperatures and high humidity as well.

2. Other species in captivity

It would be impossible to list each and every species with all of their traits, so here is a short list of just a few of the species in captivity you can find:

Indian Flower Mantis
Dead Leaf Mantis
Orchid Mantis
Arizona Unicorn Mantis
Gambian Spotted Eye mantis
Common Mantis
Spiny flower mantis
European Mantis
Thistle Mantis
Egyptian Pygmy Mantis
Carolina Mantis
Borneo Mantis
Devils Flower Mantis
Wandering violin mantis

Chapter 3: Your Pet Praying Mantis

If you have decided to keep a praying mantis at home as a pet, then you also need to learn about the different sources to find a pet mantis. These creatures are not only available in the wild but are also bred because they are in demand in pet trade and also because they are valued highly in farming and in agriculture.

This chapter will tell you everything that you need to know about the various sources for mantises and other will also give you other important information that will help you prepare for your very own praying mantis.

1. Why mantises make great pets

Besides being considered mystical creatures, there are several other reasons why mantises came to become some of the most insects as pets. Here are some reasons why bringing mantises home can be extremely fulfilling:

- **They are very interesting creatures**

    Praying mantises are extremely interesting to watch. For the most part it may seem like the mantis is just staying still for hours on end. However, this is actually part of the mantis' hunting strategy.

    In the wild, a praying mantis will lie low and will be absolutely motionless until any prey wanders past them. When it does, the mantis lashes out in a split second, grabs the prey with the front legs that have the spikes to keep the prey in place and secures its food.

    This behavior is very interesting to watch even when you have a pet mantis at home. You can feed them with live insects from time to time and watch this incredible hunting behavior unfold before your eyes.

- **They are extremely docile**
The aggressive hunting behavior may have you thinking that the mantis is not really the right pet for you. However, even though these creatures are extremely aggressive, they are surprisingly friendly towards their owners.

A praying mantis is a large insect, which also means that it is quite easy to handle. They can also be tamed quite easily. Once they are tame, they will readily crawl on to your palm and will love being in your company.

It is very rare that your praying mantis will try to bite you. As long as you know how to handle your praying mantis correctly, you can be sure that there will be no accidents, as these creatures are quite calm and docile.

The only concern when it comes to handling a praying mantis is when you handle an adult. Since they have wings, they may just fly away if they are not in the mood to be handled. As for the younger mantises, you can handle them without any hassle.

When you are interacting with an adult praying mantis, make sure that you keep all your doors and windows secure so that there are no chances of the mantis escaping.

- **It is like entering a whole new world**
When you have a praying mantis as a pet, it is like you have a mini zoo at home. The enclosure of the insect is a whole world in itself.

Then, you can watch your pet grow, hunt, molt and even become a mature insect. If you wish to breed these insects, it is also an extremely rewarding experience that you certainly do not want to miss out on. You will actually get to watch the whole life cycle of this beautiful insect. For those who love to watch life go by, the praying mantis is one of the most fascinating pets that you will ever have. If you love to watch an aquarium, for instance, then watching a praying mantis is ten times better.

- **Easy to keep as pets**
The praying mantis is one of the easiest pets to have at home. All you need to make sure is that your mantis has a good enclosure that is safe and somewhat similar to his natural environment. Building a mantis enclosure is also a great experience.

Then, you do not have to worry about food bowls, water bowls or even giving your pet constant attention. As long as the praying mantis is fed well, he is quite capable of keeping himself entertained and entertaining you in the process.

However, the more you handle your praying mantis the tamer he will get. Spending a few minutes getting your praying mantis out of his enclosure and just watching him crawl around is very soothing.

Now that you know how wonderful a praying mantis can be as a pet, the next question is where to source one from. There are various options. You can buy your mantis from a breeder, look for one in a local pet store, ask a fellow mantis owner if he or she has any nymphs that you can take care of or you could catch one yourself.

The next section of this chapter tells you in detail how you can find a praying mantis that you can bring home as your pet. You can choose the option that is most convenient for you.

2. Where to get a mantis from?

The best options when it comes to buying a praying mantis is to look for a breeder or to catch one yourself. Catching a praying mantis can be quite tricky, but the next section will fill you in on all the details that you need to know to catch one safely.

Buying from breeders

There are some breeders who rear mantises mostly for farming or agriculture purposes. If you know of anyone who owns a praying mantis, you can speak to them about local breeders. You also have the option of buying from breeders online.

The biggest disadvantage with buying online is that most mantises do not survive the trip from the breeder's to your home. So, unless you are able to find a local breeder, it is best that you do not purchase a nymph or an adult praying mantis from online breeders.

The other option when it comes to buying from breeders is to buy an entire egg case and then hatch it in your home yourself.

When it comes to egg cases, you can also look online for "Praying Mantis Egg Case sets" They come equipped with everything from the housing to some sample food for your nymphs.

These kits are put together as starter kits and are meant to encourage children to be responsible pet owners. You can get one for yourself, too and begin your journey as a praying mantis owner.

Getting an egg case

The egg case, also known as the ootheca, is normally packed in a plastic cup when you buy it from a breeder or when you pick up a set for yourself.

The first thing that you need to do is find a good habitat for the egg case so that the nymphs have a safe environment to hatch into.

Tips for the habitat:

- Your mantis nymphs require an enclosure that is clear and well ventilated. That way they get enough light and heat as well.
- The habitat should not have any gaps or holes that the mantis can escape from.
- The nymphs are extremely small, almost as small as mosquitoes. So, make sure that the enclosure is really sealed off.
- You can purchase these enclosures online. You will be able to find one that is specifically for praying mantis nymphs.

Keep the egg case warm
Normally the eggs are laid in winter and will remain dormant through the cold months. Therefore, it is necessary to allow the egg case to warm up a little before they hatch. This can take a couple of weeks.

Tips to keep the egg case warm
- The egg case should be kept away from any direct sunlight and draft in order to keep it intact.

- Usually, in the wild, the egg cases are attached to plants or twigs in order to keep them warm. You can do the same by placing a few twigs inside the enclosure and putting the egg case between them.

- If you are unsure of what kind of plant to use, you also get artificial egg case holders that are perfect for keeping the egg case warm.

- The enclosure should be kept humid. This means that you will have to mist the enclosure once every day to provide enough moisture for the egg case.

- After the egg case is placed under the right conditions, you will have to wait for about 3-10 weeks for it to hatch depending on the species of praying mantis.

Getting ready for the hatchlings
- When you wait patiently, you will see that dozens of nymphs will hatch out of the egg case.

- When the nymphs are emerging from the egg case, make sure that you do not touch or disturb the habitat. You do not want to injure the nymphs if the case rolls or falls.

- When they hatch, the nymphs are extremely delicate, so make sure that you do not touch them, as you may injure them.

Releasing the nymphs
- It is a good idea to release most of the nymphs when they hatch.

- In about 3-4 days of hatching, it is a good idea to release 3-4 nymphs out into a garden or suitable habitat.

- For the rest of the nymphs that are in your current habitat, make sure that you leave plenty of foliage and sticks for them to feed on.

- Make sure that you feed and take good care of the nymphs.

- You must be willing to care for your nymphs every single day to ensure that they are healthy.

Feeding the nymphs
- When your nymphs have hatched, you need to provide them with ample food to ensure that they thrive.

- They need to be fed with soft-bodied insects such as fruit flies once every three days.

- Mantises should be fed consistently. Making sure that they get enough food will help ensure that they do not display any form of cannibalism.

- The habitat should be kept humid for them to thrive.

- It is necessary to mist the habitat every week to keep the humidity at the necessary levels.

- When the mantises grow into juveniles you can give them larger insects such as crickets to eat.

Releasing mantises
- If you are unable to provide consistent care for the praying mantis for their whole lifetime, it is a good idea to release them into the garden after they develop wings.

- If you wish to keep them as pets, it is recommended that you only keep one or two and release the rest.

- There are chances that your praying mantises will take refuge in your garden, where you can watch them everyday.

- When releasing your mantis, look for different plants that are infested with soft-bodied insects so that your mantises have enough food.

FAQs about egg cases
If you have bought an egg case from a breeder, then you may have several questions about caring for the cases and ensuring that your mantises are healthy.

Here are some frequently asked questions:

- **How many days does it take for the egg case to hatch?**
  It typically takes between 3 to 10 weeks for the nymphs to hatch out of the egg case. This depends entirely on the species of the mantis. You need to be patient and make sure that your mantis egg case gets the right environment to thrive in.

- **What do I do after the egg case has hatched?**
  Take the habitat of your egg case outside. Release most of the nymphs that have hatched and only keep about 3-4 of them for you to observe. You can typically raise only a few of them until adulthood, so it is best to release most of them.

- **The weave of the enclosure is larger than the nymphs. What if they escape?**
  If you are using a woven mesh to cover your habitat, make sure that you choose one with the smallest holes. However, you do not have to worry about nymphs escaping because they have long legs that prevent these seemingly small creatures from escaping.

- **Why is it important to release young mantises after they hatch?**
  By nature, a praying mantis is a carnivore. If you do not give them ample food, there are chances that the nymphs begin to feed on each other. The stronger ones will feed on their weaker siblings to get their nutrition.

- **Is a praying mantis a predator?**
  As discussed in the previous sections, praying mantises are among the fiercest predators. They will eat just about any live bug that they are able to capture. One bug that they do not really feed on is the ladybug because it has a rather bitter and foul taste.

- **Should they be provided with food while in the habitat?**
  Yes, you need to make sure that the nymphs have enough live insects and bugs to feed on in order to prevent any form of cannibalism among them.

- **What should praying mantises be fed?**
  Praying mantises can be given any insect that they can catch easily. This includes aphids, baby mantis flies and fruit flies.

- **How often should a praying mantis be fed?**
  In the case of praying mantis nymphs, you should feed them every 2-3 days.

- **Do the nymphs need any water?**
  Praying mantises do not require any water. All the moisture that they need is absorbed from the insects that they feed on. They also derive moisture from the plants in their habitat. All you have to do is mist the habitat regularly.

- **Can praying mantises fly?**
  Although they can fly, they have very poor flight. Praying mantises also walk and move quite slowly. Even after releasing them in the garden, you will find them around the same spot for several weeks.

- **Why are twigs and plants needed?**
  The egg case needs twigs and plants in order to stay warm and protected. After they have hatched, praying mantises need a good perch, which can be provided by adding as many leaves, twigs and plants inside the habitat.

If egg cases are not easily available to you, the next option that you have is to catch a praying mantis. While this is relatively easy to do, it can get tricky if you are not sure of the right way to do it. The next section tells you in detail how you can catch a praying mantis and bring it home as a pet.

Catching a praying mantis

Praying mantises are relatively common creatures in most backyards and gardens within their natural range. This includes most places with a warm and humid environment.

If you are planning to catch your own praying mantis, then you will have to learn all that you can about the right places to find these elusive creatures and the best way to catch them without harming them.

The only thing that makes it quite hard to catch a praying mantis is the fact that these creatures are masters of disguise. They have the ability to camouflage themselves so well that it becomes almost impossible to find them.

In this section we will give you a step-by-step process to find the mantis and then catch him correctly.

Attracting praying mantises to your garden

The first thing that you should do is make sure that there are enough praying mantises visiting your garden or living in order to catch one to keep at home as a pet.

If you are lucky enough to have a good population of praying mantises in your garden already, then you can go straight to catching one. However, if you have looked for a praying mantis and have not really been successful in your pursuit, you may have to attract them to your garden first.

Here are some things that you can do in order to attract more praying mantises to your garden:

- There are certain plants that tend to attract predatory insects like the praying mantis. The more of these plants you have in your garden, the more likely you are to have a good praying mantis population in your garden. The plants that normally attract mantises are cosmos, angelica, marigold, yarrow and raspberry canes. You can also try growing caraway, dill, fennel and other culinary herbs that these insects enjoy quite a bit.

- Opt for pest control methods that are organic. It is best that you do not use chemical-based pesticides if you are trying to attract mantises into your garden. These chemical-based pesticides even kill the useful insects like praying mantises.

- Place shallow dishes around your garden with some pebbles in them. Fill the dishes with water enough to cover the bottom of these pebbles. There are chances that a praying mantis will visit your garden to cool off in one of these bowls.

- Make sure that they have enough shelter and protection. During the day, mantises will require protection from predators like larger insects and also birds. It is a good idea to grown plants that are short, such as oregano and thyme. This will give them enough shelter. You can also add a layer of cut leaves, mulch and stray on the soil to make a cozy shelter for praying mantises.

- Spray the plants in your garden with insect attractants that are commercially available. Most of these insect attractants are organic and will therefore not harm any of your plants. If you wish to, you can also make an insect attractant at home. All you have to do is mix one part of whey yeast and one part of brewer's yeast with 10 parts of water and spray it on your plants.

Finding and catching mantises

Once you have made your garden an attractive place for insects like the praying mantis, the next step is to actually catch them. Here are the answers to some questions that you may have about catching a mantis.

- **Where can I find praying mantises?**
The most important thing to do is to look for a praying mantis in the right place. Here are some tips to make it easier for you to find a praying mantis in your garden:

    - Praying mantises prefer areas that have woody plants and flowering shrubs.

    - Make sure that you look very closely, as these creatures camouflage themselves really well and blend in with their surroundings. If needed, you can also use a magnifying glass.

    - It is best to check in areas that are humid and rich in greenery. Find places where you are likely to find plants with some moisture around them.

    - You can also look in places that have several bugs and insects. Mantises will gather in these areas to find their prey.

    - If you have seen a praying mantis in your garden before, look in the same spot several times.

- **Should I take any precautionary measures?**
Praying mantises are aggressive predators and may attack when caught off guard. The good news is that praying mantises are not really poisonous, so even if you do get nipped by one when you are trying to catch it, there is no need for you to worry.

In any case, it is a good idea for you to wear a glove that is normally used for gardening in order to stay protected from the bite of these insects.

If you do get bitten by a praying mantis, all you have to do is shake your hand up and down rapidly. This will lessen the pain quite a bit.

Praying mantises also have very strong legs with sharp spikes on them. Therefore, you need to be very careful when you catch a praying mantis. There are chances that your hand or finger may get poked by the several spikes that are found on the forelegs of this insect.

You also have the option of using a net that contains very small holes if you are planning to catch an adult mantis. This will keep you safe and will also make sure that the mantis does not get injured in the process.

- **How do I handle the mantis?**
When you are picking up the praying mantis you need to make sure that you are extremely cautious. There is a correct way of handling the praying mantis if you want to make sure that there are no injuries to the insect. Here are some tips the handle the praying mantis correctly:

- When you pick up a praying mantis, make sure that you pick him up around the abdomen. You can also pick him up around the thorax.

- You must not squeeze the insect too hard. If you are not comfortable picking him up with your fingers, you can also use forceps to catch him gently.

- The abdomen of the praying mantis is located just behind his legs.

- The area between the middle legs and the front legs is the thorax.

- No matter what you do, make sure that you do not get your fingers too close to the forelegs of the praying mantis, as you may get pinched by the spikes or he may try to grab your finger.

- **Where do I keep the mantis after catching him?**
  You need to make sure that your insect does not escape and must also provide him with a temporary container that is safe for him. Here are some useful tips that will help you keep your mantis safe until you shift him to his permanent enclosure:

  - Use a large, empty jar that can hold at least 16 ounces of fluid.

  - The best option is a peanut butter jar or a pickle jar that has been cleaned well.

  - Use a transparent jar so that you can keep an eye on your mantis.

  - Using a plastic jar is recommended, as it is less likely to break.

  - Once you have placed the insect inside the jar, place a cling wrap on the mouth of the jar and secure it with a rubber band.

  - Punch several holes into this cling wrap to ensure that your mantis gets enough air to breathe.

- This jar is only a temporary enclosure for your mantis. You need to set up a full-fledged habitat to make sure that your mantis thrives and stays healthy.

Once you have caught your praying mantis, you need to learn the correct way to handle him and interact with him. Praying mantises are quite docile and are also quite easy to tame when you decide to bring one home as a pet.

3. Taming your mantis

The idea behind taming a praying mantis is to make sure that he is comfortable being touched and handled. After all, when you bring any insect home as a pet, you would like to spend as much time with him as possible and also get him in and out of the enclosure.

Taming a praying mantis also ensures the safety of people who want to interact with him. A praying mantis that is comfortable being handled is less likely to attack. As mentioned before, the bite of a praying mantis is not really harmful but can be quite painful.

Here are a few simple steps to tame your pet praying mantis:

- Start by putting your hand out to your mantis. Just place your open palm near the door of the mantis enclosure and wait for your mantis to walk on to it.

- Do not try to grab the mantis when you are trying to tame him, as you will only scare him away.

- When you allow the mantis to walk on to your palm, you make him believe that your palm is a safe place to be on.

- If the mantis does not come to you as soon as you place the palm at the opening of the enclosure, wait for a few minutes. If he is still hesitant, place a small piece of meat on your palm and he will come for it.

- Try this everyday until your pet mantis is comfortable walking on to your palm without any treats.

- Once your mantis is comfortable, you can start taking him out of the cage gently.

- There are chances that your insect may get startled or afraid. This will make him want to fly away from you.

- If you feel like the mantis is going to jump or fly, just use your free hand to shield him from doing so.

- You can also use your free hand to feed your mantis. While he picks up his food to eat, gently stroke him.

- If the insect gets scared or shocked, try again after a few hours or just hold off for a day.

- Once you have fed the praying mantis and pet him for a while, put him back in his enclosure.

Follow these steps everyday consistently if you want your mantis to be entirely comfortable being handled by you. Using treats or food is a good idea, as the mantis will then begin to associate your palm with food and will come to you readily. He will also stop perceiving the hand as a threat and will be happy to interact with other people as well.

4. Can you keep them in groups?
One of the most important things to remember is that it is never a good idea to keep more than one praying mantis in a single enclosure. Praying mantises are cannibalistic. This means that they will eat one another at times when more than one mantis is kept in an enclosure.

If you wish to keep more than one praying mantis at home, it is a good idea to keep them in separate enclosures. Even if they are kept in the same enclosure, it is mandatory to place screens to provide each mantis with his own separate space to thrive in.

That said, why do praying mantises exhibit cannibalism? This behavior is mostly seen in females after mating. They are known to bite off the heads of their mate. In addition to that, cannibalism is seen in captivity when the praying mantises are not well fed. They tend to eat the weaker ones in the enclosure as a means to obtain nutrition.

Cannibalism in mantises
Sexual cannibalism is most prevalent in praying mantises. After the male mounts the female and deposits his sperm, it is very common that the female ends up eating the male. This is surely not out of anger and aggression. In fact, it is an attempt to create better offspring.

Recent studies revealed that cannibalism in praying mantises has evolved over time as this behavior helps the female provide for the offspring. The male becomes a source of nutrition for the female and thus the offspring in a way.

A study conducted Katherine Barry from Macquarie University in Australia and William Brown from the State University of New York, Fredonia was published in a journal named the Proceedings of the Royal Society.

To conduct this study, male mantises were fed with crickets that had been given doses of amino acids that were radioactive. A group of mantises were allowed to breed. Half of these pairs were separated after mating and the other half were left to be devoured by the female.

Then the flow of these radioactive proteins was studied in the body of the females that were cannibalistic. The flow of these proteins through the eggs also was studied.

According to William Brown, "the production of eggs increased in females that exhibited cannibalism." In the wild, not all males are eaten by the females after mating. Only between 12-28 percent of mating acts end in cannibalism. For females that do exhibit this behavior, it is seen that almost 63% of the diet of the female is made up by the male.

This cannibalistic behavior is actually beneficial to the species by helping the female produce more eggs. The increase in the number of eggs is not immediate. However, it has often been observed that cannibalistic females tend to store the sperm for fertilization later on.

In one breeding season, females can lay several clutches of eggs. Having the male sperm stored in the female's body means that she can fertilize them later and therefore, have more clutches in a single breeding season.

In the wild, male mantises often choose females that are well fed to prevent this behavior. This was proven by a study that was recently conducted on male mantises.

The male mantises were given three different options to choose from in order to carry out any form of interaction. The first option was a female mantis holding food, the second one was a male mantis holding food and the third one was an empty handed female who could potentially be hungry.

The male mantis chose the female with food in her hands as she was most likely to be well fed and therefore, the chances of being devoured would be much lesser for the male.

In captivity, if you want to prevent any cannibalism, it is a must to separate the male and female immediately after mating. You must also make sure that you give your mantises enough food to prevent this sort of behavior. The best thing to do, however, is to have only one mantis per enclosure. If you wish to breed your mantises, you can introduce a female later on.

Which species can be kept in groups?
While most species exhibit cannibalism and tend to be aggressive, the ghost mantis is considered to be more communal in nature. Even if the ghost mantises do not have as much food available, they are least likely to attack each other.

The ghost mantis is known to be very quiet and non-aggressive. If you want to keep ghost mantises in a group, it is best to keep those that are similar in size in one enclosure to further reduce the chances of attacks. You must also make sure that they get enough food such as fruit flies to stay healthy and to prevent any fights.

5. Praying Mantis Shedding

There is very little you can do when it comes to praying mantis molting. The more undisturbed the mantis is, the better. However, learning about molting will give you a chance to provide the right conditions for your mantis to thrive in. Here is a detailed explanation of the molting process to help you prevent any bad molt that can lead to serious health issues for your praying mantis:

- **How do you know when your mantis is close to a molt?**
  This is actually quite simple to know. The first thing that you will notice is that the mantis becomes very disinterested in food. The mantis will prefer to simply sit at the top of the housing area or will remain on the perch, hanging upside down. Even when they have moving prey in the cage, the mantis will ignore it.

  Even when you try to hand-feed the mantis using a pair of tweezers, he will simply bat it away. In case your mantis has already developed wings and is still showing no signs of hunger, chances are that your mantis is approaching old age.

The other thing that you will notice is that the mantis will stay still in the exact same place for days on end. If it is not molting season, the mantis may still roost at the top of the enclosure and may even hang upside down. However, he will keep switching places through the day. They are most likely to change their positions at night, which clearly shows that these creatures are nocturnal.

Since there are very few predators around at night, they prefer to move around during this time. The third and final sign that your mantis is molting is that he will turn pale. This is the result of the old skin loosening up and the new skin emerging from underneath. The mantis will begin to show absurd body movements such as quivering and shaking to help push the old skin out and make way for the new one.

- **How to manage the molting stage**
The molting stage is one of the most important stages in the life of a mantis. In case the molt is not successful, it can have serious repercussions on the mantis' health. For instance, there are chances that he will get stuck in the old skin while he is pushing.

If he stays in the old skin for too long, the old skin will harden and the new skin will grow over it, leading to disabilities in the mantis and, in worst cases, death.

You will need to provide your mantis with something that he can hold on to during this stage. This will help him get out of his old skin easily. If the mantis falls during this process, it dies in a day or two.

Mantises rarely survive a fall, but if the height that they fall from is very low, they still have a chance to survive.

Once the molt is complete, your mantis will stop eating. During this time, you need to ensure that you do not leave any prey insects inside the cage. This can make your praying mantis itself a target for these prey insects.

When he is molting, the mantis is extremely weak. He will need at least 24 hours to get rid of the old skin. Therefore you need to ensure that you do not disturb him when this process is taking place. You can leave the mantis without any food for even a day or two after the molt is complete.

- **Why is molting important?**
With every molt, the size of the mantis increases dramatically. In 4-6 months, the mantis will reach adulthood. After the molts during the 2nd and 3rd week are complete, your mantis may also develop wings.

When a mantis is fully mature, shedding stops. They will use the wings to fly in some cases or may even use them to showcase some threatening behavior.

- **How to make the molt successful**
There is no way you can guarantee a successful shed. However, there are some tips that you will find useful to help you manage the shedding season easily:

- The enclosure should be misted at least once a day to make sure that the environment is moist enough to help him get rid of the old skin easily.

- You must not feed your mantis a few days prior to shedding. This helps reduce the size of the abdomen, allowing him to slip out of the old skin easily.
- The mantis should be handled well before the shedding season to keep them strong and in shape for when it happens.
- The container must not be moved around.

6. Praying Mantis FAQs

Praying mantises are not common household pets. At least, they are not as common as dogs or cats. Thus it is best that you read up and learn about these creatures as much as you can before you bring one home.

As you learn about praying mantises, you will find yourself asking more questions about providing the right kind of care for your fascinating new pet. Here are some common questions that are asked by individuals who are new to the world of praying mantises:

- **Is a praying mantis toxic to dogs and cats?**
  This is a very common question as most people who wish to keep smaller pets may also have other household pets such as cats and dogs at home.

  As many books and websites would tell you, praying mantises are extremely aggressive predators. They will try to catch any living being that unwittingly crosses their path. That said, praying mantises are also very easily scared by large creatures. So, you can rest assured that your dog or cat is not really at risk when he is around the praying mantis.

  In case the dog or cat startles the praying mantis, he might nip the animal. This sting, although painful, is not poisonous to your dog or cat. All you have to do is rub the area that has been stung vigorously to reduce the pain.

The biggest concern with most pet parents is the dog or cat eating the praying mantis. This is quite likely to happen. The praying mantis is not poisonous, but the dog or cat may develop some gastrointestinal irritation because of the spikes on the legs of the praying mantis. If this happens, it is best that you take your cat or dog to the vet immediately.

- **Do praying mantises make good pets for children?**
Yes, praying mantises do make great pets for children, as they are quite easy to take care of. In fact, several schools include praying mantis terrariums as part of studying different ecosystems and teaching children to engage with smaller creatures.

That said, you need to make sure that the child is supervised when he or she is caring for a praying mantis. The good news is that praying mantises do not have to be fed every day and do not need long walks like other pets. The only thing that you need to teach your child is how to handle the mantis correctly in order to prevent any bites or nips.

You will also have to help the child with different things such as temperature settings of the enclosure, the humidity and cleaning the enclosure. It is best that you allow a child to have a pet praying mantis when he or she is about 11 or 12 years of age.

- **How long do praying mantises live?**
The life span of a praying mantis depends entirely on the species. Usually, the larger varieties of praying mantises tend to live longer than the smaller ones. It is also common for females to live longer than males.

When you have bought nymphs or hatched them from an egg case, it will take about 4-6 months for them to become fully mature, depending on the species. Once they have reached adulthood, they may live for between 3-8 months, again, depending on the species.

The better care you provide for your mantis, the longer they will live. If you do not feed your mantis too often and also make sure that the temperature and humidity is maintained as required, you can increase the lifespan of your mantis. One of the biggest problems and causes of death with pet mantises is overfeeding. As long as you give them enough food, as often as needed, they are bound to live longer.

- **Are there any legal considerations with keeping mantises as pets?**
In some states of the United States of America, keeping any exotic species as pets is illegal. This may also include the tropical species of praying mantises. You can, however, keep praying mantis species that are native to the region that you live in without any hassle.

In some counties like New Zealand and Canada, you cannot keep any tropical insects as pets. There are several rules and regulations around keeping praying mantises as pets in certain European countries as well. This mostly includes species that have to be imported. Most of these countries do not allow the import of live animals, which automatically makes it illegal to have a species that is not native to the country.

So if you are planning to bring home a praying mantis, it is a good idea to check for the different legal limitations that may prevent you from having one at home as a pet.

- **Why is my mantis not eating?**
Mantises shed their exoskeleton or skin periodically. This process is called molting, which is quite normal for most insects. During

this phase, it is common for the mantis to stop eating a few days before he sheds.

In case your mantis is not eating even though it is not molting season, then it is a good idea to offer some different kind of prey for him to eat. In any case, a mantis not eating is not really any cause for concern, as these insects can live almost for 2 weeks without eating anything.

- **How do I know if the mantis is molting?**
  We will talk about molting in detail in the following chapters. However, here are some simple indicators that tell you that your mantis is all set for the molting season:
  - He will stop eating and will hang upside down.
  - A thin, whitish layer is seen on the body of the mantis.
  - The wing buds, which are located in the area that the wings sprout from, will become swollen when a nymph is becoming an adult.

- **Can praying mantises harm their owners?**
  It is very rare that a praying mantis would harm the owner. However, in some cases, bites and grabbing of the finger have been reported by mantis owners.

This usually happens when the mantis thinks of your fingers or your hand as prey. This is also only possible when the mantis is large enough to actually grab your finger.

You can just pull him away from your finger if this happens. A mantis bite need not worry you, as it is completely non-poisonous. Of course, it does sting quite a bit. All you have to do is shake your hand when you are bitten and apply some ice in the case of swelling.

- **How to tell if a mantis is an adult**
  Whether you are buying mantises or hatching them at home, you need to be able to tell the difference between a nymph and an adult. This is especially necessary if you plan to breed your praying mantis. Here are some differences between nymphs and adults:
  - Nymphs will never have wings. An adult mantis may or may not have wings depending upon the species, although this is very rare.
  - Size does not indicate age in the case of mantises. They do grow as they age. However, in some species the adults grow only to about 1 inch in length while other species can be as large as 4 inches in length.

- **How to tell if the egg case or ootheca is fertilized**
  If you are planning to buy an egg case and hatch it at home, you need to know if it is fertilized or not. If not, then your egg case will, obviously, not hatch. In some cases, the egg case is produced by the female even though it has not been fertilized.

  Unfortunately, there is no way of telling if your egg case is fertilized or not. All you can really do is provide the best possible care for your praying mantis egg case and hope that they hatch in a maximum of 10 weeks' time.

The next step is to ensure that your praying mantis is getting the right care and housing conditions to thrive in. This is the best way to improve the life span of your mantis and make sure that he is happy and healthy.

Chapter 4: Praying Mantis Care

You need to make sure that your praying mantis has the right living conditions to thrive. They need a good enclosure that mimics their natural environment and they also need the right food in order to stay healthy.

It is quite easy to provide for praying mantises, as they are the least demanding type of insects. This chapter will give you all the information that you need in order to give your praying mantis the perfect place to call home.

1. Housing

Mimicking the natural habitat of a praying mantis is actually quite easy. You can construct a great enclosure for your praying mantis with a few basic items that you can find in and around your home.

Here is a complete guide to creating the perfect habitat for your praying mantis to live in.

The right height

In the wild, praying mantises will spend most of their time hiding in bushes and trees. They are seldom on the ground. Therefore you need to make sure that your praying mantis enclosure is the right size. Typically, your praying mantis cage should be twice the height of your praying mantis at least, and here is why:

- Praying mantises, as mentioned above, are arboreal. They need to have enough space to climb. This could either just be the sides of the cage or even the plants, branches or twigs that you have added into the cage.

- Molting is a very important developmental stage in the life of a mantis. The enclosure should have enough space to molt properly. Without this, the mantis may even be left disfigured. In some cases, it can also make them incapable of hunting and feeding.

- Improper molt is one of the primary causes of death in praying mantises.

- When they molt, praying mantises require a decent height that they can attach their rear legs to. Then the old skin splits and just slides off down their back.

- If the mantis does not have enough space for the skin to slide off, he may fall off from his perch in the middle of this process. The result of this is that the body shape of the mantis will become odd. In some rare cases, the mantis may not survive an improper molt.

Ensure it is escape proof

Praying mantises are great climbers, so it is necessary to ensure that the cage is fully escape proof. You will need to find a lid that is tight fitting, especially for the younger mantises. The air outlets should be very small, ensuring that the mantis cannot fit through it.

The space should stay humid

Humidity is also very important for the mantis to be able to molt properly. If the enclosure is too dry, they tend to struggle to release the old skin, leading to several health issues.

Therefore, when you choose an enclosure for your praying mantis, make sure that it can retain the humidity. For this reason, a glass or plastic enclosure is more suitable than one that is made from mesh.

While humidity is very important for mantises to thrive, the cage should also have proper ventilation. Mantises require fresh air. In addition to that, a cage that is humid and warm can lead to the growth of mold. As a result, you need to have some option for ventilation such as small holes on the lid or on the side. These holes should be small enough to keep your mantis from escaping.

The enclosure should allow easy temperature control
Most species of praying mantises will be able to cope even at room temperature during the warmer months. You need to provide additional heat during winters. At all times, the ideal temperature within the enclosure is 25 degrees C.

The cage that you choose must be easy for you to heat. As a result, it is best that you opt for glass and plastic cages as they tend to provide better insulation and also trap heat better during the colder months.

Provide easy access
When you make any enclosure for a pet, the most important thing is that it must be easy for you to access. After all, you need to feed your pet and also clean and maintain the enclosure.

The most important thing, of course, is that you should be able to get your mantis in and out of the enclosure easily. You definitely want to have as much interaction with him as you can while he is with you. This can only be achieved if you have an enclosure that allows easy access.

The best option is to have one with a top lid that you can open and close as needed.

The cage should provide visibility
This, of course, is for your benefit. The best thing about having a mantis as a pet is being able to watch him climb, catch his prey and just go about his daily routine. A clear glass or plastic enclosure serves this purpose perfectly.

Different kinds of praying mantis enclosures
There are various kinds of enclosures that you can choose from for your praying mantis. The perfect one depends upon the size of your

mantis. In the case of baby mantises, they are not more than 1 cm in length. On the other hand, the adults can grow up to 10 cms in length.

If you place a baby mantis in an enclosure meant for an adult, chances are that you will never be able to see the baby mantis. As a general rule of thumb, it is best to keep the smaller mantises in the smaller cages and the larger ones in the larger cages.

So, if you are planning to hatch mantises at home or want to raise them from the time they are nymphs, you should also be prepared to provide up to 3 different sized cages through his lifetime.

Only when the mantis is large enough will you have to invest in a proper enclosure. With the smaller ones, you can use several household items to keep them.

Cage options for baby mantises

There are several options that you have with baby mantises that you can find in your home. Here is a list that you can choose from, along with tips to make the enclosure suitable for the nymphs.

- **Plastic cups and jam jars**
  - You only need a clear plastic cup or a clean jar to keep mantises when they are little.

  - Cover the mouth of the cup or jar with a muslin cloth or any net material. Use a rubber band to secure it in place.

  - The muslin cloth allows proper ventilation for the mantises and also keeps them from escaping.

  - This covering will also become a great perch for your little mantis and you will often see him hanging upside down at the mouth of the jar or cup.

- **Cricket tubs**
  - This is one of the most popular options for housing mantis nymphs.

  - You can easily source a cricket tub from pet stores that also sell various types of reptiles or other exotic pets.

  - This is an inexpensive caging option for your praying mantis and is also very easily available.

  - Cricket tubs also provide enough ventilation through holes that are either cut out on the lid or on the sides of the tub.

  - The only issue with a cricket tub is that it is not tall enough to accommodate a growing mantis.

  - In order to make it more suitable for your pet, place the tub vertically, instead of horizontally. Then, you can line the actual base of the tub (the wider side) with the substrate, usually tissue paper.

  - This way, you have an enclosure that is tall enough and the nymphs also have a wall line with paper to climb up and down.

- **Transparent Tupperware**
  - This is a popular option, although it can turn out to be quite expensive. If you have some lying around in your house, this is the best option for you.

  - A Tupperware box is used exactly like the cricket tub. The only thing that you will have to do is make some holes in them to allow proper ventilation.

- The best way to do this is to melt these holes into the box with a hot pin or use a soldering iron.

Cage options for larger mantises

When your praying mantis is large enough, you can move him to a "proper enclosure". This gives you a good view of your pet and also gives the mantis the right habitat to live in.

The best part about these enclosures is that you can get as creative as you want and make one that looks extremely attractive. The different enclosure options for large praying mantises are as follows:

- **A terrarium**
    There are several terrariums available online for praying mantises. You can also build one yourself if you wish. We will discuss this in detail in the following section. Here are the top benefits of using a terrarium.

    - **Well ventilated:** You can add a mesh door to the top of a glass aquarium to make a roof for the enclosure. This not only keeps it well ventilated but also allows very easy access.

    - **Option of front doors:** If you purchase a terrarium online, they usually come with a front door that you can lock. This keeps your mantis from escaping and also gives you easy access. Locked doors also means that you can keep your pets or children from opening the enclosure accidentally.

    - **The base is deep:** Most aquariums and commercially available terrariums have a base that is deep. This makes sure that the substrate stays in place and that your mantis has a thick floor to rest on when he wants to.

    - **Easy heating:** These terrariums are made from fiberglass or glass, which allows you to heat them very easily. All you have to do is place a heater under the terrarium and set it to the temperature that you want inside it.

- **Easy to accessorize:** A terrarium will give you a lot of space to work with. This means that you can add light units, twigs, branches, commercially available perches and a lot more to make the cage look beautiful and also make the habitat suitable for a mantis.

- **Sweet jars**
These large containers are perfect for holding your mantis. You can also build a terrarium inside these jars. Here are some tips if you wish to keep your mantis in a sweet jar:
  - You can buy your sweet jar from any local sweet store. The best part is that they are very economical.

  - The downside with these jars is that they do not provide easy access like the terrariums.

  - Make sure that you find some way to ventilate the enclosure. You can use muslin cloth or net just like the jam jars that you used to keep the baby mantises in.

- **Glass or plastic tanks**
This is yet another option that is extremely easy to find in local pet stores and aquariums as well.
  - The only thing that you need to consider with these tanks is enclosure. Some of them may even come with a lid that has large holes, which need to be covered.

  - The best way to cover the holes on the lids of these tanks is to use a plastic bag.

- An escape proof lid might be required in case you decide to bring home one of these tanks for your praying mantis.

Now that you have the suitable options for an enclosure, the next step is to make it suitable for your praying mantis to live in. The next section tells you how you can convert these enclosures into a haven for your beloved pet praying mantis. With these tips, you will be able to create an environment that is identical to the natural habitat of your mantis.

Creating the perfect living conditions
Once the right enclosure is available to you, you need to make sure that you create the perfect environment for your mantis. There are some factors that you need to take care of in order to help your mantis thrive in his housing area.

- **Humidity**

    You do not really have to provide your mantis with any drinking water in a bowl. When they are kept in a terrarium or enclosure, mantises prefer to drink water from the small droplets that form on the wall of the enclosure.

    For this to happen, you need to make sure that the enclosure is humid enough. It is best to mist the inside of the enclosure using a spray bottle. Avoid using any spray bottles that you have used before to prevent the chances of chemicals getting into the housing.

    Buy a new spray bottle and make sure that you use it only for your mantis cage to ensure maximum safety. You will have to spray the insides of the enclosure every few days. The water on the walls is good enough for your mantis.

    When these water droplets evaporate, they will also provide your mantis with ample humidity. That brings us to the right humidity inside the enclosure. There are some points that you should keep in mind to make sure that the humidity is just right:

- Your mantis will need about 60-70% humidity inside the enclosure for proper molting and to be healthy.

- If the enclosure has more ventilation holes, you will have to mist the insides more often.

- It is a good idea to use a hygrometer to measure the relative humidity inside the enclosure.

- The hygrometer is marked from 0-100% humidity. It measures relative air humidity, which also calculates the humidity based on the temperature. You see, as temperature increases, the water vapor and the air tend to expand.

- You can also improve the humidity of the enclosure by adding a substrate that retains water. Spray water onto this substrate regularly to keep the enclosure moist enough.

- If you notice that the inside of the cage is getting too dry, too soon, it is a good idea to block some of the ventilation holes using gauze or mesh.

- If the humidity is too high, the first thing you can do is reduce the frequency of misting.

- Following this, you can also improve the ventilation of your enclosure to ensure that excessive humidity does not lead to the growth of any form of mold.

- **Temperature**

The next most important factor is the temperature of the enclosure. Mantises are from warmer climates and will require a certain temperature in order to thrive.

Mantises are cold-blooded creatures and the body temperature is moderated as per the temperature of their surroundings. When it gets too cold, they move to warmer areas and vice versa.

In the wild, the mantis will look for the warmest and the sunniest areas during the day. As the temperature increases through the day, they will move to cooler areas in order to prevent any overheating.

When they are kept in captivity, you need to make sure that the same concept can be applied. For this reason, only one end of the cage must be heated. This gives the mantis the option of cooler areas along with a "hotspot" when it gets colder.

The heat requirement depends largely on the species of praying mantis that you have as a pet. However, in most cases, keeping the temperature at around 24 degrees C is perfect for your mantis. The cooler area of the enclosure can measure about 18 degrees C.

When you are working on the temperature of the mantis enclosure, here are some questions that you may have:

- **What heating equipment should I choose?**
There are several options available with respect to the heating equipment that is best suited for a mantis cage. Here are some options and the features of each option to help you choose better.

Heat mat
- A heat mat is a type of heating element that is flat and usually placed between two pieces of sturdy plastic.

- The thickness of these mats is about 1mm. However, you get different options with respect to the length of the heating mat.

- Of all the heating elements available, these are probably the best because they are very easy to source, they are inexpensive and are also very power efficient.

- Heat strips are a type of heating mat that are very long. This is ideal if you have multiple enclosures placed next to one another.

- You can place the heat mat just below the enclosure of your mantis. Make sure that you do not cover more than 50% of the area of the floor.

- You can alternatively attach this heat mat on the back wall of the cage.

- Heat mats may also have a peel off option that lets you stick them to the side or the back of the cage easily.

Heat cables
- Heat cables are nothing but electric cables that are available in different lengths. They become warm once they are plugged in.

- The issue that you may face with a heating cable is keeping it in place. You may require highly adhesive tapes in order to do this.

- Heating cables are perfect if you have multiple enclosures. They can all be heated at once easily, even if they are placed on different shelves. All you have to do is run the cable under the cage, along every shelf.

Heat lamps
- With heat lamps you get to light the cage up while you heat it.

- Since the enclosure is small in size, you will need a bulb that is very low in wattage. The best option is to get a 15 watt or 25 watt bulb.

- One thing that you should keep in mind with heating lamps is that the bulbs tend to get very hot. As a result, you will have to keep several safety precautions in mind.

- The most important thing to remember is that your mantis must be kept away from the heat lamp. Use a metal grill or a bulb cover. That way your mantis will not climb onto the bulb and suffer any burns.

- When using a heat lamp, you will also need to install a thermostat. That way, you can prevent any chances of overheating.

- You must also find a suitable way of installing this in the cage. The best option is to use a lighting hood that will keep the cage warm and your mantis safe.

Heating based on the room
- Another option is to place the cage in a room that is set to the temperature required for your mantis.

- You can use any spare room or a shed that is heated using a thermostat. That way your praying mantis will be comfortable all year along.

- If you do not have a room to spare, you can also buy a large aquarium that fits your praying mantis cage. Then, you can heat the larger enclosure. This method is best suited for baby mantises.

- **Why should you use a thermostat for the mantis cage?**
A thermostat helps regulate the temperature of your mantis cage. It controls the electricity flow into the heater that you choose and ensures that it does not overheat.

If you are using a heating mat or a cable, the amount of heat generated is not high. Since they are also used to heat up just one part of the cage, the chances of overheating are very low. On the other hand, if you are using a heating lamp, a thermostat is very important.

Suppose you turn on the heating lamp and have to run some errands right after. You possibly forget to turn the heater off. The temperature rises fast and in just a few hours, the enclosure can get overheated.

To prevent these situations, it is a good idea to use a thermostat. That way, even if you do forget to turn the heater off, you will not have to worry about any overheating.

You have the option of purchasing a matstat that usually goes with a heating mat. This is a very convenient option and is also quite cheap.

- **How do you heat the enclosure for an adult mantis?**
Be it an adult mantis or a juvenile mantis that is large in size, the best option is to use a heating mat. These mats warm the cage up gently and are also very easy for you to install.

If you have multiple cages or a large collection of praying mantises, you will need to use a heating cable or a heating strip.

That way you can heat up multiple cages in one go. You also save a lot on power costs.

Using a heating bulb should be your last option. Not only does it use a lot of power, it also requires a lot of precautionary measures to be taken to keep the mantis safe.

- **How to heat the enclosure of hatchlings**
The first thing about hatchlings is that they are placed in enclosures that are extremely small. If you are buying an egg case, you may also have multiple hatchlings to take care of. In that case, heating multiple jars or cups that are so small can be quite a challenge.

Here are some steps that you can follow to provide enough heat for baby mantises:

- Buy a wooden vivarium or an aquarium that is large enough to place all the baby mantis enclosures in.

- Place a heating mat under this aquarium or vivarium.

- If the environment is well ventilated, this is the perfect way to keep your baby mantises cozy and warm.

- When using a vivarium, make sure that you use a thermometer. That way you can be sure that the temperature is maintained at the necessary levels.

- Once the mantises are large enough you can place them in a proper enclosure and use any of the heating methods mentioned above.

With the above tips, you can be sure that your mantis will have the right temperature and will also be completely safe.

- **Substrate**
The used substrate can do a lot for the cage conditions. The most important function of the substrate is that your cage remains more humid. It also makes the terrarium look a lot better.

In the case of baby mantises, you can use a kitchen towel to create your substrate. You simply have to fold it to the right size and use it. In addition to this, kitchen towels make great substrate because you can just replace them when they get too messy.

In the case of larger mantises, you have several options to place as substrate. The best option is potting compost or vermiculate. You can even mix the two and place them at the bottom of the cage. This not only makes the mantis cage look attractive but also soaks in the moisture when you spray the cage. That way, it remains humid for much longer.

- **Accessories**
You do not need to add too many accessories in a praying mantis enclosure. There are some options available online when it comes to praying mantis perches and toys. You can invest in them if you are keen. These accessories will make the cage look almost like a mini jungle.

However, the best option for a praying mantis cage is dried twigs that you will find in your garden. All you have to ensure is that there are no insects on the twigs that you use that may harm your mantis. So, if you are collecting twigs from your garden for the cage, make sure you rinse them well and allow them to dry before you place them in there.

When placing the twigs in your mantis cage, be sure to trim the top of these twigs so that the cover of the terrarium fits in place. You must also keep in mind that these twigs will lead to the ventilation holes of the terrarium. If you are feeding any insects to the praying mantis that are small enough to escape from these holes, keeps the twigs shorter.

Alternatively, you can also cover the holes with mesh. That way, the live feed that you give your mantis will not be able to climb out of the enclosure and escape.

Twigs are the ideal perch for your praying mantis. They are also very useful when the mantis is molting. Twigs let the mantis climb up and down and get the exercise that they need.

Besides the twigs, you do not really need any other accessories. There are options of feeders that we will discuss in the next section. You may add them to the cage if needed.

2. Feeding

One of the best things about owning a praying mantis is watching them catch and eat their prey. You will notice that your pet mantis, who has been practically motionless for hours, will just spring into action when you feed him.

He will move his head around to keep an eye on the prey. This is when they will display the amazing feat of being able to turn their head by 180 degrees. Then, they inch towards the prey and in seconds will have a firm grasp on the creature.

Your praying mantis will need meat because it is a carnivore. They do not eat any plant material. They have a wide range of prey that they feed on in the wild. They can even eat some types of lizards and birds in the wild.

There are only two things that the mantis looks for in his prey. It should be small enough for him to hold and it should move fast enough to get the attention of the mantis. There are some instances when pet mantises have also reached into fish bowls to grab goldfish!

Things to know about praying mantis feeding

Before you move on to the type of food that you must give your mantises, you need to understand the feeding cycle and the feeding habits of praying mantises. That will help you decide what and when to feed your pet mantis. Here are some important things to know about praying mantis feeding habits:

- The requirements will depend on the gender, the stage of development, the size of the mantis, the size of the prey and the health of the mantis.

- In general, male mantises do not need as much food as female praying mantises.

- If you are feeding nymphs, then you will have to choose small insects such as fruit flies. On the other hand, if your nymphs belong to a smaller sized species of praying mantis, you may have to choose even smaller feeding options like spring tails. In the case of nymphs that belong to the larger species of praying mantises, you can give them food like houseflies right after they hatch from the egg case.

- For young nymphs, the frequency of feeding should be every 2-3 days. This is because the type of food that you give to them has lesser nutritional value.

- Young nymphs are also more active in comparison to the older ones and will, therefore, need more food.

- When the nymphs are older, you can give them larger prey such as small hoppers and roaches.

- Since older mantises are less active, you can feed them about 3-4 times a week. In the case of the mature mantises, you will only have to feed them every 5-7 days.

- When choosing the prey for your mantis, the rule of thumb is that it must not be larger than half the mantis' size until he reaches the 6th instar. In case of the pre-adult mantises, you can give them prey that is 3/4th the size of their body. Fully-grown adults will be able to catch pray that is as large as them, or larger.

- During the initial days of feeding, keep an eye on the mantis to make sure that he is actually eating. Wait for him to catch his food if you are giving him live prey. In some cases, the prey will simply escape or hide, leaving your mantis starved.

- To make sure that your mantis is eating, you also have the option of giving him food from tweezers. Then the mantis will grab the food given to him and begin to eat it immediately.

- Giving mantises prey that move fast and move a lot is the best idea.

- You have to make sure that your mantis gets a varied diet. Giving him only one kind of food will not do much for his health.

- Try to include hoppers, flies, locusts, morio worms, mealworms and more in your diet for your praying mantis.

- If you cannot include this much variety, you need to make sure that you choose a method called gut loading to make sure that they get enough nutrition. This means that you feed the prey before you feed the mantis. Here are some gut loading options with mantis prey:
  - Water, honey and bee pollen can be given to flies
  - Whilst is ideal for roaches
  - Fresh fruit and vegetables are ideal for locusts and worms.

With these tips, you are able to ensure that you maximize nutrition for your mantis to keep him healthier for longer.

What to feed praying mantises

This section will tell you about the different feeding options with praying mantises depending on the age and stage of development. The benefits of each type of food are listed. You will be able to find most of these foods with pet stores that sell exotic pets and reptiles.

Best foods for praying mantis hatchlings

When they hatch, praying mantises are just about a centimeter in size. So, you need to make sure that you give them food that is soft and also much smaller than them. The best options include:

- **Pinhead crickets**
  - These creatures are named pinhead crickets because of their size. They are nothing but crickets that have just hatched. They are either black or brown crickets.

  - These creatures measure about 1mm in size and are perfect to feed baby mantises.

  - The biggest disadvantage with pinhead crickets is that they die very easily because they dehydrate really fast.

  - When you buy a tub of these crickets from the store, you will see that most of them die in just a few days.

  - To prevent this, you can feed your pinhead crickets foods that are rich in moisture such as apples, potatoes and carrots. This will keep them alive for longer.

  - Another issue with these creatures is that they tend to stay on the ground for the most part. On the other hand, the nymphs will spend their time on the perches, away from the floor.

This means that the praying mantis will not even notice the crickets in the floor. In addition, baby praying mantises do not really come down from the perch.

- **Fruit flies**
  - These creatures are about the same size as pinhead crickets. However, they tend to live longer.

  - It is very easy for you to buy readymade fruit fly cultures from most reptile shops.

  - In about a week of purchasing these cultures, you will see that they will have hatched into dozens of fruit flies that you can feed to your praying mantis.

  - Another advantage of fruit flies is that they are likely to stay near the roof of the enclosure, making it easy for your mantis to eat it.

  - They are also easy to breed and all you have to do is put a few of them close to the baby mantis.

Although the fruit fly is the best way to go, it is a good idea to provide your pet mantis with enough variety. When you are bringing home small insects for your praying mantis, you need to make sure that you handle them well. Otherwise, before you know it, you will have a swarm of fruit flies all over your house.

There are three options available to prevent this from happening:

- **Refrigerating:** The best thing to do is to chill all your feeder insects. All you need to do is put them into the fridge about 10 minutes before you feed your mantis. This will make them a lot slower and you can handle them easily.

They will eventually gain their pace and come back to their original temperature, but, before that, you will be able to put them into the cage of your mantis and close it.

You may have to buy a small cooler or refrigerator for this, however. It is not really pleasant to have crickets in your own refrigerator. Your family may be quite uncomfortable with it.

- **Pooter:** As mentioned before, there are some feeder options for your mantis cage and this is one of them. It is a very simple device. It has two plastic tubes and a clear vessel in between.

You need to place a filter on one of the tubes. All you need to do is place one tube over the insect that you wish to catch. Then suck hard on the tube that you placed the filter on. The insect will be sucked into the collection pot.

Then, all you need to do is pour the trapped insects into the mantis cage. This device is a lot more effective with crickets and you can catch dozens of them in one go.

- **Stealth and larger cases:** This is certainly the easiest method available. If you are raising egg cases, especially, this method will really come to your rescue.

The disadvantage of using this method is that you put the mantis nymphs at a reasonable amount of risk. So, if you have a very small amount of these hatchlings, this may not be the way to go.

This technique is normally used by breeders who raise several ootheca at once. You will need a large cage that you will fill with several twigs to give the mantises several climbing options, such that they avoid one another. The twigs should be arranged to form a maze of sorts.

Then, take a fruit fly culture and bang it hard on a surface like a table. This will get all the fruit flies to the bottom. Then, before the flies are able to respond, place the mouth of the culture near the opening of your mantis cage and shake the culture to let the fruit flies in.

Following this, dozens of these flies will fall into the cage. This gives your baby mantises an endless supply of flies that you just have to top up once in a while.

If you want to use this method with your pet baby mantises, it is best that you wait for them to become about 2-3 cms in size. Then, you can place them in individual cages and then follow this method to feed them.

Best foods for adult praying mantises

When praying mantises grow, they are extremely easy to feed. This is because they become more resilient when they are grown. Their prey is also larger and a lot easier to handle.

All you will have to do is grab the prey with a pair of tweezers and let them into the enclosure of the praying mantis. Here are some options to feed your adult praying mantis:

- **Crickets**
  - You have different types of crickets that you can feed your praying mantis, including black, brown and silent crickets.

  - You can buy them in different stages, starting from younger crickets to the large, black cricket adults.

  - The best thing about crickets is that you will always find a variety that is the perfect size to feed your mantis no matter how large or small he is.

- This makes crickets one of the most popular feeding options for a praying mantis.

- However, they tend to stay closer to the ground and seldom climb up to the mantis, making it a major drawback.

- In addition to this, the adult crickets also tend to chirp all night long, making them quite annoying.

- In some rare cases, they will also escape the enclosure and lodge themselves behind furniture and become hard to find.

- **Locusts**
    - Locusts are another top favorite when it comes to feeding praying mantises. Again, they are available in a variety of sizes that suit your praying mantis.

    - The biggest advantage with locusts is that they do not make as much noise as the crickets.

    - In addition to this, these insects also get really large and are a very meaty option for the larger varieties of praying mantises.

    - Locusts also climb up the twigs and the sides of the cage. They also like to perch on the twigs in the enclosure.

    - This makes it more likely for them to come into contact with your praying mantis, who can feed on them easily.

    - Most praying mantis owners will also tell you that these creatures are a lot easier to handle.

- They are much slower and are not as jumpy as crickets. So, if you prefer to pick up the prey to feed your praying mantis, this is the best option available for you.

- **Waxworms**
  - A waxworm is a caterpillar of a wax moth. These insects are plump and extremely juicy, making them a favorite of the praying mantis.

  - It is also great that they pupate when left in the cage long enough. When they turn into moths, they also make great prey for your praying mantis to catch from the perches.

- **Mealworms**
  - The thing about mealworms is that they are not really worms. They are actually Tenebrio beetles that are in the larval stage.

  - Several studies conducted on mealworms show that they are not really nutritious. However, they are really easy to handle.

  - These worms make a great option if you want to give your praying mantis a break from the regular crickets and locusts.

  - You do not have to worry about running out of enough food for your praying mantis if you have enough mealworms on hand. When you run out of crickets or locusts, they make the perfect meal.

- **Blow flies**
  - These mid-sized feeder insects are great for your praying mantis. If you are buying these maggots, do not purchase them from fishing stores, as they may contain chemicals. It is best to get them from a pet supplier.

- You can just leave these maggots in the enclosure of your mantis in a small pot with some sawdust.

- They will pupate in this setting and you can just sprinkle the pupae on to the substrate of the mantis cage.

- The flies will hatch in a while and will become the best flying prey for your mantis.

- Because you are inserting the pupae, this is also the easiest type of live feed to handle.

The best part about raising mantises is that you never run the risk of overfeeding. You can give them as much food as you want, the more the better in fact.

Giving your mantis a lot of food in the younger stages of development helps them mature into adults faster when compared to those that have been placed on a stricter diet.

It is a good idea to keep live food available to your baby mantises at all times. When the praying mantis does not want to eat or does not want to be disturbed by the live feed, he will simply retire to the top of a perch or to the roof of the enclosure.

When your mantises are grown, it is best to place them in different enclosures and maintain a good feeding chart. This will help you keep track of how often you need to feed your mantis and when they are ready to molt.

All you have to do is remove any half eaten food from the cage every day. For the most part, praying mantises will eat every single day. When they start to lose interest in food, it is a sign that the molting season is on the way.

During this period, you can just withhold the food for a few days until they are done with molting.

3. Cleaning

Cleaning a praying mantis cage is quite simple. All you need is a temporary enclosure for your mantis. You can use a jar that is the right size for your mantis to do this. Empty out all the twigs from the enclosure and rinse them thoroughly. You can also get fresh twigs that need to be washed and dried before placing them in the enclosure.

Then, you will have to clear the substrate out and wash the entire enclosure. Make sure that you only use plain water and scrub out the debris, if any.

Chemicals in the detergents can harm your mantis quite a bit and can even be fatal, so it is best that you avoid it altogether. Allow the enclosure to dry out in the sun so it is also disinfected.

Layer the clean enclosure with the substrate of your choice, then place the twigs back in place. Use a thermometer and a hygrometer to make sure that the temperature and the humidity are right. You can heat the enclosure to the necessary temperature and also mist it slightly to ensure that the environment inside the enclosure is just right.

After the enclosure is set up, release your mantis into it. Let him settle down. Once you put the mantis back in, wait for a few minutes and try to feed him.

Daily cleaning tip: If you find any half eaten or uneaten pray at the bottom of the enclosure or on the twigs, make sure that you clean it out. Decomposing prey can cause infections and may also lead to a foul smell in the enclosure.

4. Free-range mantises

It is also possible to have free-range mantises in your home. This means that the mantis will not be placed in an enclosure. Before you decide to do this, make sure that your entire family is comfortable with the idea. When you are certain, there are a few options for you to keep your mantis without any enclosure indoors.

- **Purchase a potted plant:** You will need to buy an individual plant for each of your mantises, as they are known for being cannibalistic. Choose a plant that is tall enough to allow your mantis to climb easily. The pot should not be too large so that your mantis can find any food at the bottom easily. Here are a few pointers for buying a plant for your mantis:
  - Make sure that the leaves on the plant are very wide. That way, your mantis will have enough space to hide from the sun and can also rest when he wants.

  - When you are planning to keep a mantis free range, look for a species that does not develop wings. Then, there are no chances of him escaping.

  - If you are choosing a circular plant, make sure that the diameter of the pot is thrice the length of the body of your mantis. In the case of a square or rectangular pot, the width should be twice the width of the mantis' body and the length should be thrice the size of the mantis' body.

- **Place the pot correctly:** The best place to keep the plant is the windowsill. That way the plant will be able to get enough sunlight and will be healthy. If the windowsill is not an option, choose any other place where your plant will get enough sunlight. You must make sure that the plant is out of reach from any of your other pets and children who are too young.

- **Feed your mantis:** You will have to purchase or collect enough insects with soft bodies to make sure that your mantis has enough to eat. When you are feeding a free-range mantis, look for prey

that will not fly away. Here are some pointers to help you feed your free range mantis:
- It is a good idea to make food available at all times to your mantis if he is kept in a cage. However, when the mantis is kept free range, you must ensure that you keep an eye on his feeding schedule.

- Make sure that there are no fallen leaves at the base of the pot or on the soil so that your mantis does not have any place to hide in.

- Pick the food that you want to give your mantis with a pair of tweezers. Offer it to your mantis and watch him grab on to it immediately.

- **Creating the right environment:** Your plant should be kept in a room that is warm. The soil and the leaves should be misted frequently to keep the right humidity for your mantis. You need to watch the soil carefully to ensure that it does not become dry. Here are some things to keep in mind with creating the perfect environment for your mantis:
  - If you notice that a portion of the pot is getting dried up too soon because of prolonged exposure to sunlight, then it is a good idea to frequently turn the pot to keep the soil moist.

  - Your mantis does not really require an additional source of water, as the misting and the moisture from the prey are good enough. However, if you feel concerned that your mantis may not get enough water, you can also place a small bowl near the pot for your mantis.

5. Keeping mantises in your garden

If you are unable to keep mantises indoors for various reasons, you can always create a whole world of mantises in your garden. Here are some simple steps to have a garden that is thriving with praying mantises:

- **Buy an egg case:** The first step is to do some research about the type of mantis that you want. Then, you can purchase an egg case for the type of mantis that you prefer. It is a good idea to buy multiple egg cases. Here are some tips for buying an egg case:
  - With each egg case, you can get between 50-200 nymphs, so buy as many cases as you require based on the size of your garden.

  - On average, a single mantis egg case is enough to populate a garden with an area of 1666 sq.ft.

  - Plant several egg cases around your garden and wait for them to hatch.

  - Once they have hatched, the baby mantises will scatter on their own. You will have to really keep an eye out, as mantis nymphs are very well camouflaged and can be hard to find.

  - Watch the weather before you plant the egg cases. If it is too cold, it is a good idea to wait until the weather gets warmer to hatch your egg cases.

  - If you have to delay the process of hatching your egg cases, make sure that they are stored properly.

  - The egg cases should be placed in containers that have enough air circulation. Then, they can be refrigerated until the weather is warmer.

- **Planting the egg cases:** Planting these egg cases is quite easy and here is a breakdown of how you must go about it:

- Collect several twigs and tie each egg case gently to them using a wire, zip tie or any twine.

- Make sure you handle the egg case well to prevent any damage.

- Look for areas that are slightly elevated, with enough cover to make sure that the egg cases are hidden from predators.

- Secure these twigs to fences or to any branches that are low.

- These egg cases will contain slits that the baby mantises emerge from. Make sure that the slits are not facing inwards when you are tying the egg case to the twig.

- Do not use any sticky tape or glue to attach the egg case to the twig. These sticky substances can damage the nymphs and the egg case, too.

- **Allow the egg case to hatch:** It will take up to 10 weeks for the egg cases to hatch. You can take a few measures to ensure that the egg cases hatch successfully:
  - Mantises thrive on moisture and humidity, so it is a good idea to mist the area around the egg cases to help them hatch faster. You must also mist some of the leaf cover so that the mantises have enough water to drink when they emerge.

  - If your garden has enough insect life, you will not really have to worry about feeding your mantises.

  - Each generation of praying mantis has a life cycle of about 1 year. They will usually die when the cold weather approaches.

- However, with the right conditions, female mantises will lay egg cases in the warmer months to make sure that your garden is always thriving with mantises.

Most mantis owners also begin to breed mantises as a hobby. If you want to breed your mantis, too, the next chapter will give you all the details that you need.

Chapter 5: Breeding Praying Mantises

Breeding a praying mantis is not only fun but is also extremely rewarding. However, in comparison to other insects, they are quite hard to breed. If you plan on breeding praying mantises, you need to have more than one pair of males and females that will mature at around the same time.

You also have to take good care that the female does not eat the male well before they actually mate. You also need to make sure that you take good care of the egg case that is laid by the female. This is called ootheca and you need to take really good care to make sure that the nymphs that hatch are healthy.

The only issue that you will face with respect to breeding mantises is that the care can differ quite drastically from one species to another. While some species are very easy to breed, others require a good amount of experience for you to be able to breed them.

1. Finding a male and female mantis pair

In the case of some species of insects like the stick insect, the female does not require a male in order to fertilize the egg. However, almost every species of praying mantis will require a male in order to fertilize the pair. The first thing you will have to do is tell the difference between a male and female mantis.

Difference between male and female mantises

Learning how to distinguish between a male and female mantis will help your breed them successfully. There are two methods that will allow you to understand the difference between the two genders:

1. Segment counting method

When the mantises are older than the fourth instar, you will be able to tell the difference between the male and female with this method. However, the ease of telling the difference depends upon the species of mantis. If the mantis species is small, you will require a magnifying glass in order to tell the difference. Here are some tips to use this method to distinguish between the two genders:

- The rule of thumb is that female praying mantises have 6 segments in the abdomen while the males have 8 segments.

- The last segment in the case of the female mantises is a lot larger than the male. The male will have more segments, as the abdomen tapers to an end.

- In order to count the number of segments, you need to look under the mantis.

- It is much easier to use this method in the case of an adult mantis because the body is larger.

- These segments differ as per the species. For instance, in the case of a Chinese mantis, the segments not only differ in shape but in size as well. The male not only has more segments at the end of the abdomen but also differently shaped ones.

1. **Sexual dimorphism**

   Sexual dimorphism means that the male and female of the same species have distinct physical characteristics that allow you to tell the difference between them.

The level of sexual dimorphism varies between species of animals. For instance, it is really high in the case of peacocks and quite low in the case of species like horses.

In adult praying mantises, the difference becomes more evident when they reach the L5 or the L8 instar. Of course, this also depends on the species. There are some parts of the mantis' body that look distinctly different based on the species. To check for sexual dimorphism, you can check the following.

- **Antennae**
  - In the male praying mantis, the antennae are thicker and longer in comparison to the females.

  - This difference becomes more evident when the mantises reach adulthood. As the nymphs grow into adulthood, the antennae also continue to grow steadily.

  - When you are trying to tell the difference between a male and female, it is useful to know that the antennae of the female are thin and hair-like.

  - One unique characteristic of the antennae of the male in the case of the family Empusidae is that the male has antennae that look like feathers, while the antennae of the female are smooth.

- **Body size**
  - In some species of mantises, there is a very obvious difference in the size of the body between the male and the female. Two such examples are the Budwing Mantis and the Orchid Mantis.

- If you are raising nymphs, you will notice that some of them continue to grow while the others stop growing after a while. The former are the males and the latter are the females.
- The difference in the body size becomes even more evident when they are adults.

- **Body type**
    - The body of the male praying mantis is more slender in comparison to the body of the female praying mantis.
    - When you look at the thorax, this difference becomes even more evident.
    - In most species, the area near the thorax is very evidently wide in the case of the female. In the case of the female dead leaf mantis, for instance, the shield on the back is much larger.
    - The difference in the body type, too, becomes more evident as the nymph grows into an adult.

- **Wing length**
    - The wings sprout only when mantises reach adulthood. Therefore, you can only see this difference in adult mantises.
    - In males, the wings tend to grow longer in comparison to the females.
    - In fact, the length of the wing is much less than the length of the body in females. However, with males, the length of the wing may easily overshoot the length of the body.

- The reason for this difference is that males need to fly in order to look for their mate. Females, on the other hand, have a heavier body that does not allow them to fly as much.

Finding a mantis pair

When you are looking for a pair of mantises, here are a few pointers that will help you find a pair that is likely to have a higher rate of success in breeding:

- Make sure that the female and the male are at the same stage of development.

- An older male mantis is unable to mate with a female mantis, making the pair unsuccessful.

- In some species, you can get a male that is just a few weeks older or younger than the female and still be sure that they will breed successfully.

- Even if the male and the female hatch from the same ootheca, they may not be at the same stage of maturity. In many cases, even before a female from the same egg case reaches maturity, the male may die due to old age.

Putting the couple in the same enclosure

Once you have found a pair that is likely to be successful, you need to make sure that they are put in the same enclosure correctly. The following steps will prevent cannibalistic behavior between the male and the female quite significantly:

- Make sure that the male and the female are at least 2 weeks old.

- You need to feed the male and the female well to prevent cannibalism.

- They need to be shifted into a larger enclosure. Remember, the larger the enclosure, the better it is.

- Whenever you find the female facing the male, make sure you turn her the other way around such that the male watches her.

- The female should be fed with large prey animals like crickets.

- Make sure you do not disturb the pair.

- Keep an eye on the behavior of the female. She should not demonstrate any aggressive behavior toward the male. This includes behavior like striking the male, moving towards him or turning towards him.

- You should also make sure that the male is not trying to escape the female. He must not move frantically or try to fly away.

- If you see any of the above behavior, make sure that the pair is separated immediately.

- Even after the male has mounted the female, he may take several hours to actually mate. Leave them undisturbed.

- Once you see that the male has dismounted, you should get him out of the enclosure immediately.

In species that are not too cannibalistic, such as the Ghost Mantis, you can leave the pair in the enclosure even after mating.

You will never be able to tell if the female has been fertilized. Sometimes, even when she has not been mated, she may lay the egg case or the ootheca. Once the spermatophore from the male have been processed by the body of the female, you will also see the spermatophore leaving her body in the form of small, white secretion for several days after they have mated. However, you can still not be sure if the mating was successful.

A female praying mantis will stay fertilized for the rest of her life after she has mated once. It is a good idea to find her a mate only after she has laid at least 4 ootheca.

Ensuring the male stays alive
One of the biggest issues with mantises is that the female tends to eat the male after mating. Sometimes, she may showcase this cannibalistic behavior even before they have mated. You need to make sure that you do not allow this to happen or you must just deal with the natural behavior.

If you want to keep the male mantis alive, here are a few steps that you can follow:

- Make sure that the female has been fed really well before you introduce the male to her.

- As soon as the male has been introduced, provide a prey item for the female to feed on.
- Use a large container to place to pair to make sure that the male has some place to escape. A male mantis will be aware of the intention of the female.

- You need to ensure that the male and female mantises are calm when they are introduced. They should never be handled too much before introducing them to each other. This makes them quite stressed.

- It is a good idea to introduce the male to the female in the evening instead of in the evening.

If you plan on breeding several pairs of praying mantises, you need to make sure that not more than 10% fall prey to the female's cannibalistic behavior. The female can be fertilized even if she kills the male during the mating process.

2. Hatching the eggs

Mantis eggs come enclosed in a pouch that is foamy in appearance. This is known as the ootheca, an egg case or an egg sack. When the ootheca is just produced, it is very soft to touch. However, over time, it becomes firm, dry and rough.

The egg case keeps the eggs protected until they hatch. The size, shape and color of this egg case changes depending on the species. In some cases there are a few eggs in this egg case while other species may have hundreds of eggs in a single sack.

This egg case is laid in fall in most species. The adults normally die immediately after laying the ootheca. The eggs that are resting inside the ootheca stay in this state until spring. After this, the nymphs hatch and then go on to lay the next generation of egg cases.

Caring for the eggs

As mentioned before, the adults will die after the ootheca has been laid. This means that you will have to take care of the egg case. Even when the adults are alive, there are few things that you need to take care of when you are looking after the eggs:

- The female should not be disturbed for at least 3- 5 days after she has produced the egg case.

- After this, the egg case can be removed from the enclosure of the female, as they are hard enough to be handled.

- It is a good idea to remove the egg case from the female enclosure, as the nymphs require an environment that is quite different from the female.

- There are also chances that the female will feast on the nymphs hatch.

- The egg case should be placed in a container that is a little more than 8X15 cms in size. This allows the nymphs enough space to move around after they have hatched.

- You can manage in smaller spaces with the smaller species of praying mantises. However, a larger enclosure is always recommended.

- You need to make sure that the enclosure is well ventilated. You can use a net or make some holes on the lid of the container.

- Place the ootheca inside this container. The orientation of the ootheca should be exactly the same as the orientation that the female originally laid it in.

- You can tie the egg case with a twine to a twig.

- In the case of some species of mantises, a diapause is necessary. A diapause is basically a pause in the development of the ootheca in the colder months.

- In order to hatch the praying mantis eggs, you need to maintain the right temperature and humidity inside the container.

- Using a substrate such as small pebbles, white sand, paper and cloth is the best option for mantis eggs.

- The nymphs will hatch later on when the temperatures rise.

- One example of a mantis species that requires a diapause is the European Mantis, which is quite commonly found in captivity.

- When temperatures are low, the development of the nymphs is arrested and when they are high, development is triggered.

- If your species of mantis requires a diapause, you will have to keep them at temperatures as low as 12-15 degrees Celsius. This temperature should be maintained for a period of 8 weeks at least.

- Then you can place the ootheca as mentioned above. Normally, the mantises that are native to tropical areas will not need a diapause, as they do not experience drastic changes in temperatures and seasons.

Once the nymphs hatch, you will have to take care of them to raise them into adults that can continue the life cycle.

Caring for the nymphs

Mantis nymphs are very tiny. This is why you need to make sure that you take good care of them. You must never use any glue to secure the egg case to the twigs. This can get them caught in the glue and be injured. In some cases, they may also get trapped in the mesh of the enclosure.

You must make sure that you give the nymphs prey that is the right size. Soft-bodied and small creatures like fruit flies is the best idea.

When nymphs are younger, they are not as cannibalistic in nature. Therefore, it is possible to keep nymphs together in the same enclosure. You just need to ensure that they have enough space to hide if needed and also enough food to prevent cannibalistic behavior.

When the nymphs are older, you need to make sure that you place them in different containers. This ensures that the chances of survival are maximum.

3. Life cycle of praying mantises

The life cycle of a praying mantis is quite interesting to understand and watch as well. In order to signify the different stages of development, L-numbers are used. This is used by most entomologists and biologists. Each L-number is also called the instar.

For instance, L-1 is the first instar when the praying mantis is just born. Then the mantis moves on to the second instar or L-2 when the mantis sheds his skin.

The praying mantis life cycle contains the following different stages:

- **Eggs**
  - This is the stage that occurs just before winter sets in.

  - Females lay between 100-400 eggs immediately after she is fertilized.

  - These eggs are laid in a case that is liquid in the beginning and then hardens eventually.

  - The egg case is laid on a stem or on a leaf. As mentioned before, it is called an ootheca.

- **Nymphs**
  - When they just hatch, the nymphs normally stay close to the egg case for some time.

  - This is when they are most likely to eat one another if they belong to a cannibalistic species.

  - Then, these nymphs spread out and then look for insects like fruit flies to feed on.

- The nymphs go through a series of development stages that are also called instars. These stages of growth are repeated.

- At every instar, the nymph will shed the exoskeleton in order to increase in overall size and also to develop segments on the body.

- Before the nymph moves on to a new stage of development, it is common for him to molt or shed the exoskeleton at least 6 times.

- In the wild, most nymphs do not survive as they are susceptible to being eaten by predators such as bats, spiders and birds.

- **Adolescents**
  - Adolescents are slightly larger in size in comparison to nymphs.

  - One characteristic of adolescents that differentiate them from the adults is the fact that they molt very regularly.

  - Just before they molt, mantises become extremely sluggish and will not feed very well.

  - Molting normally ends when the warmer months begin and when the mantis matures.

- **Adult**
  - When mantises are fully grown, they are between 1-6 inches in length.

  - They come in various sizes depending upon the species.

- Normally mantises live for about 6 months to a year after which the life cycle is completed.

One of the most rewarding experiences is watching your nymphs hatch from an egg case. Then, they will continue the life cycle when given all the right temperature and environmental conditions.

Chapter 6: Health Issues in Praying Mantis

Although the lifespan of your Praying Mantis is between 6-8 months, you need to make sure that the mantis is maintained in top condition to ensure good breeding and to also prevent any fatal health issues.

One of the biggest health issues with Praying Mantises is an improper molt. Ensuring that they have the right environment for a good molt can help solve most health issues. Molting or shedding is the main health concern with mantises while there may be other issues that we will discuss in the next section of this chapter.

1. Praying Mantis Shedding

There is very little you can do when it comes to praying mantis molting. The more undisturbed the mantis is, the better. However, learning about molting will give you a chance to provide the right conditions for your mantis to thrive in. Here is a detailed explanation of the molting process to help you prevent any bad molt that can lead to serious health issues for your praying mantis:

- **How do you know when your mantis is close to a molt?**
  This is actually quite simple to do. The first thing that you will notice is that the mantis becomes very disinterested in food. The mantis will prefer to simply sit at the top of the housing area or will remain on the perch, hanging upside down. Even when they have moving prey in the cage, the mantis will ignore it.

  Even when you try to hand-feed the mantis using a pair of tweezers, he will simply bat it away. In case your mantis has already developed wings and is still showing no signs of hunger, chances are that your mantis is approaching old age.

The other thing that you will notice is that the mantis will stay still in the exact same place for days on end. If it is not molting season, the mantis may still roost at the top of the enclosure and may even hang upside down. However, he will keep switching places through the day. They are most likely to change their positions at night which clearly shows that these creatures are nocturnal.

Since there are very few predators around at night, they prefer to move around during this time. The third and final sign that your mantis is molting is that he will turn pale. This is the result of the old skin loosening up and the new skin emerging from underneath. The mantis will begin to show absurd body movements such as quivering and shaking to help push the old skin out and make way for the new one.

- **How to manage the molting stage**
  The molting stage is one of the most important stages in the life of a mantis. In case the molt is not successful, it can have serious repercussions on the mantis' health. For instance, there are chances that he will get stuck in in the old skin while pushing.

  If he stays in the old skin for too long, the old skin will harden and the new skin will grow over it, leading to disabilities in the mantis and, in worst cases, death.

  You will need to provide your mantis with something that he can hold on to during this stage. This will help him get out of his old skin easily. In case the mantis falls during this process, it ascertains death in a day or two.

  Mantises rarely survive a fall, but if the height that they fall from is very low, they still have a chance to survive.

Once the molt is complete, your mantis will stop eating. During this time, you need to ensure that you do not leave any prey insects inside the cage. This can make your praying mantis itself the target for these prey insects.

When he is molting, the mantis is extremely weak. He will need at least 24 hours to get rid of the old skin. Therefore you need to ensure that you do not disturb him when this process is taking place. You can leave the mantis without any food for even a day or two after the molt is complete.

- **Why is molting important?**

    With every molt, the size of the mantis increases dramatically. In 4-6 months, the mantis will reach adulthood. After the molts during the 2nd and 3rd week are complete, your mantis may also develop wings.

    When a mantis is fully mature, shedding stops, too. They will use the wings to fly in some cases or may even use it to showcase some threatening behavior.

- **How to make the molt successful**

    There is no way you can guarantee a successful shed. However, there are some tips that you will find useful to help you manage the shedding season easily:

    - The enclosure should be misted at least once each day to make sure that the environment is moist enough to help him get rid of the old skin easily.

    - You must not feed your mantis a few days prior to shedding. This helps reduce the size of the abdomen, allowing him to slip out of the old skin easily.

- The mantis should be handled well before the shedding season to keep them strong and in shape for when it happens.

- The container must not be moved around.

2. Signs of health issues in Mantises

If you notice the following, then your mantis could be suffering from certain health issues that you need to take care of right away:

- The mantis is not eating
- The predatory reflex seems to be slower than usual
- The mantis stays on the floor of the enclosure
- The mantis seems to be limping
- Soreness in the eyes
- The mantis is stationary even at feeding time
- The mantis is not breathing properly.

3. Causes for health issues in Mantises

The following factors play a very significant role in your Mantis' well being, so make sure that you follow the tips mentioned in the previous chapters to prevent them from harming your pet:

- **The type of water you use in the cage:** When spraying the cage of the mantis, make sure that you use spring water, distilled or filtered water. Tap water may contain chlorine, fluorides and several other components that lead to death or illnesses in the mantis.

- **The temperature of the enclosure:** The temperature should neither be too high or too low. If the temperature drops suddenly, there are chances of illnesses in the mantis, although some species are more tolerant than others when it comes to temperature fluctuations. Make sure that the internal temperature of the enclosure is appropriate for the species of mantis that you own.

- **The humidity of the enclosure:** Humidity should be maintained within the range required for mantises. If the humidity is too high, there are chances of fungal and bacterial infections in the enclosure, which can harm your mantis. One of the biggest causes for improper molting or shedding is improper humidity within the enclosure.

- **Mold:** Any growth of mold in the enclosure is harmful for the mantis. It is commonly caused be the remnants of the insects that you feed your mantis. Make sure that the enclosure is cleaned regularly. You can also use UV light to sterilize the enclosure.

- **Lack of drinking water:** While you do not have to place a water container for your mantis as such, you need to ensure that he has enough water droplets available to drink. That said, the size of the water droplets also matters. If the drops are too large, they can easily drown a nymph. When you spray, make sure that the droplets are even and small.

- **Hunger:** Do you feed your mantis often enough to prevent him from going hungry? You can increase the time frame between each feeding session to up to once every 2-4 days when he is younger. For older ones, you can keep the time frame of about 7 days. Starvation can lead to death in your mantis.

- **The type of feeder insects:** There are some insects that are poisonous for your mantis such as earthworms, stink bugs and ants. Only stick to the ones that are recommended for your mantis to keep him safe.

- **The food that you feed the prey insects:** What you feed your feeder insects matters. If they are fed with poor food, they may become sick themselves and spread the infections to your mantis.

- **Collecting feeder insects:** It is best to give your mantis cultured or store bought feeder insects. If you are collecting them from the outside, they may contain insecticides, pesticides and even parasites that can harm your mantis.

4. Common health issues in Mantises

Here are the common health issues in mantises and tips to prevent them:

Explosion
Mantises can over eat to a point where the abdomen ruptures if they are given too much food in one sitting. Make sure you restrict the amount of food that you give them to prevent this from occurring.

Vomiting
Mantises can vomit if they have had excess water. The color of the vomit will determine the cause. If the vomit has a red tint, it is due to overfeeding of fruit flies. When it is chunky and brown, it could be the result of poor quality feeder insects. Vomit with an acidic smell and a black tinge is due to fungal and bacterial infections.

Frass
Sometimes, mantises tend to have issues with passing food. This is caused by the type of feeder insect provided. For instance, some of them can drastically slow down the metabolism. This includes waxworms and superworms. On the other hand, flies can speed up metabolism. The right kind of feeder insect will provide the roughage that is needed to keep metabolism intact. If the digestive system or the anus is blocked, it can cause death in the mantis immediately.

Prolapsed anus
The digestive system of the mantis can protrude out at times. If this happens, reduce the quantity of the feed. You must also provide the right level of humidity required. This problem is usually fixed when the mantis molts.

Eye rubbing

Sometimes, you will notice that the eyes of the mantis look strange. Their face may hit the enclosure, causing a black mark or even blindness in extreme cases. If this happens, you cannot do much to help your mantis. The only thing you can do is avoid this condition in the first place. It is common when you have multiple mantises and they can see each other through the glass. The dividers should be opaque and the mantises should have enough space to move around without having to get into each other's way.

Mites

Mites are easily transferred to mantises through the feeder insects. While the mites are usually removed when the mantis molts, an infestation can lead to several problems. In some cases, the mantis is covered by so many mites that he is unable to move his limbs to catch his pray and eat. This will eventually cause death by starvation. Make sure that you store your feeder insects under suitable conditions, free from grains that is usually the cause for a mite infestation.

Egg binding

In some cases, even a fertile female does not lay an ootheca. This is because she is probably egg bound. This condition is normally caused by variation in feeding schedules, improper humidity levels, improper temperature within the enclosure and other variables that may even lead to death. During the breeding season, provide the females with water through a dropper or syringe each day to prevent egg binding. Although the reason is unknown, providing flying feeders like flies has been known to prevent egg binding.

Amputation

If the mantis gets caught in any material such as Velcro or tape inside the enclosure, he may amputate his limb to set himself free. This is fixed with molting and is not any cause for concern unless the mobility of the mantis is compromised. If this happens, you may have to cut the next highest joint with a pair of sharp scissors. While you do this, make sure that your mantis is distracted with some food.

The management of health issues in mantises is quite simple. As long as you provide the appropriate conditions within the enclosure and ensure that your mantis has ample food and water, you will be able to prevent most of the health issues mentioned above.

Conclusion

When you decide to bring home an exotic pet like the praying mantis, you can never learn enough about it. The more you understand the requirements, the better care you will be able to provide to your mantis.

Thank you for choosing this book. Each chapter has been laid out with great care to ensure that all the important details are covered, so be it a beginner or someone with experience with praying mantises, there is something for everyone with this book.

The idea is to ensure that you are fully prepared for your mantis. The species is unique and the book is designed to help you from the beginning to the end with your mantis. Hopefully, you are able to understand praying mantises better as a species with this book.

If your questions about raising mantises have been answered with this book, then the purpose is perfectly served. Here is wishing you a wonderful journey with your praying mantis.

Even though this pet is unlike any other, they can light up your world with their wonderful antics. These insects are a delight to have at home and are extremely entertaining to watch.

Make sure that you learn as much as you possibly can with each day with your mantis. You will also discover that your little fellow has a personality of his own, which will make him the most delightful companion that you can possibly have.

References

One of the best sources of gathering more information about your praying mantis is the Internet. The Internet is loaded with forums of other mantis owners, dedicated websites and a lot more to help you learn a lot about this species.

Note: at the time of printing, all the websites below were working. As the Internet changes rapidly, some sites might no longer be live when you read this book. That is, of course, out of our control.

Here are some names that are recommended especially for you:

- www.keepinginsects.com
- www.animals.mom.me
- www.usmantis.com
- www.bugguide.net
- www.wikihow.com
- www.keepingexoticpets.com
- www.instructables.com
- www.petponder.com
- www.animalsake.com
- www.theprayingmantis.co.uk
- www.thesprucepets.com
- www.exotic-pets.co.uk
- www.boards.weddingbee.com
- www.prayingmantisfacts.net
- www.livescience.com
- www.homeguides.sfgate.com
- www.pets4homes.co.uk
- www.mantisplace.com
- www.homeschool.priswell.com
- www.insectidentification.org
- www.jcehrlich.com
- www.stlzoo.org

Published by Zoodoo Publishing 2018

Copyright and Trademarks: This publication is Copyrighted 2018 by Zoodoo Publishing. All products, publications, software and services mentioned and recommended in this publication are protected by trademarks. In such instance, all trademarks & copyright belong to the respective owners. All rights reserved. No part of this book may be reproduced or transferred in any form or by any means, graphic, electronic, or mechanical, including photocopying, recording, taping, or by any information storage retrieval system, without the written permission of the authors. Pictures used in this book are either royalty free pictures bought from stock-photo websites or have the source mentioned underneath the picture.

Disclaimer and Legal Notice: This product is not legal or medical advice and should not be interpreted in that manner. You need to do your own due-diligence to determine if the content of this product is right for you. The author and the affiliates of this product are not liable for any damages or losses associated with the content in this product. While every attempt has been made to verify the information shared in this publication, neither the author nor the affiliates assume any responsibility for errors, omissions or contrary interpretation of the subject matter herein. Any perceived slights to any specific person(s) or organization(s) are purely unintentional. We have no control over the nature, content and availability of the web sites listed in this book. The inclusion of any web site links does not necessarily imply a recommendation or endorse the views expressed within them. Zoodoo Publishing takes no responsibility for, and will not be liable for, the websites being temporarily unavailable or being removed from the Internet. The accuracy and completeness of information provided herein and opinions stated herein are not guaranteed or warranted to produce any particular results, and the advice and strategies, contained herein may not be suitable for every individual. The author shall not be liable for any loss incurred as a consequence of the use and application, directly or indirectly, of any information presented in this work. This publication is designed to provide information in regards to the subject matter covered. The information included in this book has been compiled to give an overview of the subject s and detail some of the symptoms, treatments etc. that are available to people with this condition. It is not intended to give medical advice. For a firm diagnosis of your condition, and for a treatment plan suitable for you, you should consult your doctor or consultant. The writer of this book and the publisher are not responsible for any damages or negative consequences following any of the treatments or methods highlighted in this book. Website links are for informational purposes and should not be seen as a personal endorsement; the same applies to the products detailed in this book. The reader should also be aware that although the web links included were correct at the time of writing, they may become out of date in the future.

Made in the USA
Coppell, TX
03 September 2022